"I never say anything provocative"

Witticisms, Anecdotes
and Reflections by Canada's
Most Outspoken Politician

John G. Diefenbaker

Selected and Edited by
Margaret Wente

Canadian Shared Cataloguing in Publication Data

Diefenbaker, John G., 1895–
    "I never say anything provocative" : witticisms, anecdotes and reflec-
tions / by Canada's most outspoken politician, John G. Diefenbaker ;
selected and edited by Margaret Wente.

ISBN 0-88778-132-2.   ISBN 0-88778-122-5 pbk.

1. Diefenbaker, John G., 1895-   2. Canada - Politics and government - 20th
century.   I. Wente, Margaret, comp.   II. Title.

F1034.3.D5A5 1975   971.06'42'0924
F5091.5.D5A5 1975

Design: T. Wynne-Jones

PETER MARTIN ASSOCIATES LIMITED
35 Britain Street, Toronto, Canada M5A 1R7

United Kingdom: Books Canada, 1 Bedford Road, London N2
United States: Books Canada, 33 East Tupper St., Buffalo, N.Y. 14203

Contents

Introduction

1   1 "Everyone is against me — except the people!"
Diefenbaker and the Average Man

2   4 "I'm going to be premier of Canada, someday."
Diefenbaker and his background

3   13 "I've always been a House of Commons man."
Diefenbaker on Parliament

4   22 "A prisoner of success."
Diefenbaker in power

5   30 "Where, where, is the nation going?"
Diefenbaker in the Opposition

6   38 "Right here in Canada today. . ."
Diefenbaker on domestic affairs

7   49 "A gardener of democracy."
Diefenbaker on external affairs

8   58 "I never make personal allusions."
Diefenbaker on his contemporaries

9   75 "I am a free Canadian."
Diefenbaker and his principles

10   84 "I will compromise on anything, but. . . "
Diefenbaker on tradition

11   90 "If there are statesmen here, they'd better resign."
Diefenbaker on the Conservative party

12   94 "Throw the rascals in!" Diefenbaker on the Liberal,
New Democratic and Social Credit parties

13 103 "As Prince Albert goes, so goes the nation."
         Diefenbaker on the West

14 109 "Mes amis de langue français."
         Diefenbaker on Quebec and multiculturalism

15 118 "Cooperation ever, subservience never."
         Diefenbaker and the United States

16 126 "Then we have Maclean's magazine."
         Diefenbaker and the media

17 134 "As Sir John A. Macdonald said. . . "
         Diefenbaker on Sir John A.

18 140 "Nothing I ever do is political."
         Diefenbaker on just about everything else

148 A Note on the Sources

Preface

John Diefenbaker is one of the most written about Canadians in history. The number of books about him and the attention given him by the media through the years have been remarkable even for a politician of his longevity and colourfulness. What the present book attempts is to provide a sketch of the man through quotations, a medium well suited to a certain kind of portraiture.

There are scores of other sources giving the facts of Diefenbaker's career, and just as many which attempt to analyze his role in history. The purpose of this collection is more modest. It is not intended to be representative of all the issues on which Diefenbaker has spoken out over the years. And because it relies mainly on what was said for the record, what it portrays is the public man—some may say the stage character, honed to perfection in thousands of performances.

But what a performance it has been. Diefenbaker developed his style long before the days of the professional image-makers, whose job it is to package our politicians into bland, acceptable public relations men. It must be remembered that he was a boy during the reigns of Victoria and Edward VII, when politicians were among the chief public entertainers. It must also be remembered that he came to early maturity as a small-town barrister, in the days when people came from miles around to attend sensational trials for their entertainment value alone. Diefenbaker has always known how to keep his audience enthralled, and in this has taken as much pleasure as he gave. It is partly this trait which has made him unique in our time.

That he was in fact a country lawyer—more importantly, a famous defense lawyer—is obvious from the following pages. He was the type of lawyer whose job it was, when faced with condemning evidence and his client's certain conviction, to confound the jurors with his rhetoric and win them over with his wit. If sometimes, upon closer examination, the rhetoric was illogical, this was of no importance so long as it saved someone from the gallows. If the witticisms were similar for each succeeding jury—and later, for each succeeding Liberal government—no one was the wiser.

Diefenbaker has spent most of his political life in opposition, championing the cause of the underdog, a position in which he has always been at his best. That is why in this collection he seems livelier on the opposition than on the government side of the House. The roles of statesman and diplomat required of a leader in power were unfamiliar to him; the one of the rabble rouser with an ulterior motive was familiar. Indeed, he seems always to have been most at home not in the corridors of power but on the main streets in the small towns of Canada, talking with his people and giving the Grits hell.

The clearest picture to emerge from this collection is that of a man thoroughly rooted in the past, persistently having to grapple with the problems of the present. Part of Diefenbaker's love of Parliament (the subject of one section of this book) is actually an affection for the Parliament of another age. He often harks back to the time when debates tended to degenerate into vitriolic monologues and members trained in oratory never resorted to prepared speeches. Similarly, his fierce adherence to the British tradition seems a bit quaint to a generation raised on social and cultural pluralism.

He was not consistent. Despite his genuine hatred of prejudice, he has not been without a few of his own. Moreover, as this collection amply demonstrates, he often substituted petty politicking for genuine leadership. But whether or not one is in sympathy with Diefenbaker on partisan issues, one must admit that he has always been an enemy of elitism and a champion of civil liberties. More important, perhaps, he always has been, and continues to be, Canada's most quotable citizen.

M.W.

Introduction

John George Diefenbaker has lived long enough and served in our political process for more than enough time to have left the permanent imprint of his language on Parliament and Canadian politics.

This collection—chosen from his many statements, speeches, quips, ironic remarks, inconsistencies and asides—is the mark of the man.

The measure of Mr. Diefenbaker at eighty is his record not only as a giant among parliamentarians (a Canadian who saw the Westminster model as instrumental in helping set the course of Canadian identity in a hemisphere of uneasy republican governments) but of his time as Prime Minister of Canada between 1957 and 1963. In his all-too-brief period as Prime Minister Diefenbaker helped articulate Canada's distinctive national character. That was a period of Conservative rule which neither the historian nor political scientist has yet fully assessed.

In the context of postwar nation-building since 1945 Mr. Diefenbaker's populism and his sense of the Canadian identity were as essential as had been the formation of an industrial democracy and the creation of Canada's international role for the Liberal governments in power prior to 1957.

It was necessary for his Liberal predecessors to preserve, then diversify the wartime industries Canada had been called upon to raise up during the war years. A certain kind of politician and builder was required to do it, and our present status as an industrial nation in what we call in the '70s "the developed world" was assured because these governments accommodated wartime industries to postwar needs and demands.

But they did not raise up a politician or leader who could communicate to a rich nation, confident of its material success and of its large role in world affairs, that all was not well with many Canadians nor with the Canadian identity. Mr. Diefenbaker did this.

His surprise victory in June, 1957 and his sweeping one of late March, 1958, still unsurpassed in Commonwealth parliamentary history, gave expression and between 1957 and 1963 legislative response to many views we now hold commonplace.

He was suspicious of the emphasis which had been given to the maximization of gross national product and of growth for growth's sake. He saw that in a time of apparent plenty and in a society of builders and achievers there were too many deprived Canadians. He was concerned that traditional values from the land and from a multi-racial Canadian society, which he saw more clearly in populist terms than did eastern Canadian politicians, were being lost and trampled upon in our prosperity.

Looking back to what is becoming very quickly an historic time, it is uncanny how many of the public policy positions of Mr. Diefenbaker's governments of the late '50s and early '60s have become accepted Canadian attitudes in the '70s, or are still emerging from the defeats and crises on defense and economic issues which he experienced in Parliament and within his own party.

We have forgotten, perhaps, in a time of growing economic nation-alism with which successive Liberal governments have had to cope, that many of the vehicles they use to do so are based on Conservative policy and legislation, especially in the energy field. The National Energy Board which regulates Canadian energy exports to the United States and, within the terms of its act, the domestic consumption of energy, was created by a Diefenbaker government in 1959 along with the National Oil Policy in 1961. The latter guaranteed thirteen years of steady Canadian oil exports to the United States between 1961 and 1973.

Diefenbaker's successes in foreign policy as well as his defeats are reflected today in the strong views Canadians take on many world issues.

The major wheat sales to the People's Republic of China, initiated in 1959 under the Conservatives, gave later governments the oppor-tunity to use the long and mutually beneficial trade contacts with Peking in the negotiations for full diplomatic recognition of China which took place in October, 1970.

Mr. Diefenbaker's delay in supporting the United States at the start of the Cuban missile crisis in October, 1962 and his hard line against positioning U.S. nuclear weapons on Canadian soil in 1963 are reflec-ted in our current concerns over American use in this hemisphere and the new world of her still great nuclar power.

But perhaps above all, Mr. Diefenbaker as Prime Minister, and as persistent parliamentarian when he was out of office, set a new course for concern by the state for needy and chronically disenfranchised Canadians in what he saw as a superficially affluent country.

While he was Prime Minister he increased the existing federal transfer payment mechanism by about $1 billion giving these outlays the name of "Social Justice Payments".

Old age security, blind and disability allowances, unemployment assistance, hospital construction grants and the "Winter Works" programs for the seasonally unemployed were all advanced by his Conservative governments between 1957 and 1963.

The traditional Conservative policy of government as a participant in economic development rather than functioning itself as developer was put into practice, for example, with his "Roads to Resources" program which supplied government railway transport and related infrastructure to Pine Point in western Canada in the early '60s making possible the success of private enterprise there in the early '70s.

And finally when the difficult years for him came again as Leader of the Opposition and as a private Member of Parliament, John George Diefenbaker always reminded us of our common heritage in strong and simple words.

Speaking on CBC radio near the end of Expo year, 1967, perhaps the hardest year for him in his very long political life, he told us we have a heritage of "one Canada, one nation, one national idea, one national dream. . . ." In the much more stressful conditions of this decade, these things are still perhaps what most Canadians want to achieve.

In his time, John Diefenbaker has given Canadianism a new shape, much purpose and in his Bill of Rights which he considers to be his life's major accomplishment, a legislative thrust to help set us on our future national course.

John D. Harbron

You know, sometimes I think of a clever phrase during a speech and I start to say it and then I stop and think "that's taking me down a road I don't want to go" so I change direction, or don't finish the sentence. That way, they can't pin me down. They say: "Diefenbaker said so-and-so," and they go and look it up and there's a turn somewhere. They can't catch me out.

Toronto *Star* interview, 1963

1 "Everyone is against me—except the people!"
DIEFENBAKER AND THE AVERAGE MAN

I was criticized for being too much concerned with the average Canadians. I can't help that; I am one of them!
September, 1967. Speech to PC convention.

There are more votes on Main Street than Bay Street.
Peter Newman, *Renegade in Power.*

Income tax has been increased some hundred times since it was first imposed years ago and the salaried man always pays. He should be entitled to ask at this time that some consideration be given to him; for if you pauperize the salaried middle class, you destroy the bulwark on which this country depends against the isms that are sweeping the world today.
July 10, 1946, House of Commons.

A judge, with all his learning, still does not have the infallibility that is created by public opinion.
November 25, 1949, House of Commons.

It is a deep inspiration for me to see this vast audience. This is the kind of thing that gives me the strength to continue to work on behalf of the average men and women of this country. From the bottom of my heart I thank you. I won't let you down.
May 24, 1957, Vancouver.

There was no deal. There is no deal. There will be no deal. The only deal I will make will be to remove the obvious injustices against small provinces. No one can say I made a deal with anyone but the average Canadian whom I am trying to serve.
May 26, 1957, Edmonton.

The average Canadian, the men and women who work, the humble, are joining us because we have carried out our promises.

February 26, 1958, Rimouski.

I feel for those who are unemployed. I know what it means, but I promise you that as long as I am Prime Minister the humble are not going to suffer.

March 9, 1958, Edmonton.

We inherited difficulties, they cannot deny it. The people heard the story, and they had the facts and they knew.

January 19, 1959, House of Commons.

[During the Avro Arrow crisis, to the president of A.V. Roe] My stockholders are 18 million Canadians.

Thomas Van Dusen, *The Chief.*

My abiding interest is *your* interest; my guiding principle is the welfare of the Average Canadian.

From the opening telecast of the 1962 election campaign.

I want each one of you to sit down and write me your ideas and suggestions. There is no excuse for you not to do so, because you don't have to pay postage when you write to me.

March 2, 1963, Herbert, Alberta. Peter Newman, *Renegade in Power.*

I don't campaign. I just visit with the people.

1965 campaign picnic.

You have no idea what it means to come here and be addressed by my first name. I tell you, this is something that money can't buy.

April, 1962, Prince Albert. Peter Newman, *Renegade in Power.*

[A ploy to get people to stop calling him "John" after he became Prime Minister]
You never heard anyone call Mackenzie King "Willie", did you?
March 14, 1959, *Maclean's.*

From the days of Sir John Macdonald to the present, the Conservative party has been at all times the party of the average man and woman.
May 26, 1962, *Saturday Night.*

Do you really think that the Government and I would bring in anything that would harm you—the average Canadian?
June 14, 1962. Peter Newman, *Renegade in Power.*

I am not holding these meetings for headlines. I am holding them for the purpose of meeting the people and giving them certain information.
March 7, 1963, Guelph, Ontario.

I felt that if I could carry my message to the people, there would be no doubt as to the outcome.
April 2, 1963, Cowansville, Quebec.

My main political asset is that I know what Canadians are thinking.
April 4, 1963. Television broadcast.

I have been deserted and condemned. Even some of my own colleagues have left me. If they thought I would leave the helm and the Canadian people, they know how wrong they were.
March 6, 1963, Chatham, Ontario.

Everyone is against me—except the people!
Rallying cry of the 1963 election campaign.

2 "I'm going to be premier of Canada, someday."
DIEFENBAKER AND HIS BACKGROUND

Being of mixed origin myself, I knew something in my boyhood days in Saskatchewan, of the feeling that was all too apparent in many parts of Canada, that citizenship depended upon surnames, or even upon blood counts. It was then, as a boy on the empty prairies, that I made the initial determination to eliminate this feeling that being a Canadian was a matter of name and blood.

Winter, 1961, Ottawa. Peter Newman, *Renegade in Power.*

I know what discrimination is. I know how much easier it would have been for me if my name had been Bannerman, which was my mother's name.

September, 1967, speech to PC convention.

Many in Rosetown came by foot, and some by oxen. All they had were the bare essentials. Those were the days I'm glad I was privileged to participate in, days of prairie fire and drought and contaminated water, when every man was his own doctor, his own veterinarian, and provided his own entertainment.

July, 1961, Rosetown, Saskatchewan. *Time.*

I can remember being lost on the prairie one winter night in a blizzard—an experience that time does not eradicate or the passing interval make dim. My Uncle Ed and I had gone to a

school concert at Halcyonia that March night in 1909, and it
was a three-and-a-half mile sleigh drive home. We left at 10
o'clock, and we could see in the distance the light that my
father always used to put out on the door. But the horse could
not face the blizzard, and turned off. And so we were lost. We
had to spend the night in an open cutter turned up on its side.
We were lucky. The storm broke in the morning, and we were
safe.

Was I fearful of losing my life? Let me say this: it was a
frightening experience I would not like to repeat.

April, 1960, *Liberty.*

When you live in a new world—and it was a new world—you
realize something that one who hasn't had the experience
cannot realize—something of the aspirations and the needs of
the average man. We saw the opening of the west; the ar-
rival in the main of the first major influx of immigration. We
had settled around us people of various racial origins; we saw
the beginning of that Canada which we have today.

March 29, 1958, *Maclean's.*

Many of the Mounted Police stopped at our place. We lived
twelve miles from the nearest town. Everybody stopped at our
home and nobody ever paid for stopping there. The Mounted
Police used to come to our place and several of them had served
in the Saskatchewan Rebellion. Gabriel Dumont was there—
Riel's right-hand man. He had come back from exile after the
rebellion. It was only about four years ago that I learned certain things about Dumont. You know, he was the greatest
Indian fighter of all time, a man beside whom Buffalo Bill was
a novice. When he was a man of seventy-seven, I remember, he
would throw tin cans up in the air and he would hit them twice
on the way down. He had killed eleven policemen himself at
Duck Lake before he escaped to the United States.

There was one thing I could never understand and that was
the perfect part in his hair. It was a perfect centre part. About

7 years ago the Historical Review published his field notes and it was there I learned that his head had been creased by a bullet—and that explains the perfect part.

Buffalo Bill wasn't on the same street with Dumont, you know. For every buffalo that Buffalo Bill killed, Dumont had killed several.

I must say that Gabriel Dumont is a story in himself—a story that has yet to be written. It's one of the greatest stories in Canada—the story of the greatest Indian fighter of them all. His field book revealed him as the master strategist, and, indeed, had Riel listened to him rather than having paid attention to signs in the skies things might have been different, although ultimately defeat would have come. Dumont still has relatives around there, you know.

March 29, 1958, *Maclean's*.

I'm going to be premier of Canada, someday.

Prophesied at a tender age, according to family legend.

Early in the morning, at a quarter to six, when I began my newspaper-selling route, I went over to the Canadian Northern Railway Station.

There was Sir Wilfrid, in town to lay a corner stone in a church. He bought a paper. Of course I remember, because he paid me five times the value of the paper. And then we started to chat. One of those memories that I dearly cherish is that he said, "Well, let's talk together." He took me over to his private railway car. I sat on the top step, the Prime Minister on the lower step. And for three quarters of an hour we talked about this Canada of ours.

One thing I particularly remember. He stated that no matter who it was, or what his upbringing, how humble his parentage and home, he was an example of what Canada could provide. That inspired me with the idea that each of us can rise to whatever position there is in this country—provided we dedicate ourselves.

April, 1960, *Liberty*.

Well, Sir Wilfrid, I can't waste any more time; I have to sell my papers.

Laurier quoted the young newsboy's parting words in his speech the same evening.

I modeled myself from the beginning on Theodore Roosevelt. He was a remarkable man, and did more than anyone else to express the true concept of Americanism. My concept of Canadianism is modeled after that.

June 8, 1962, *Time.*

My father was making only about $600 a year, but no matter what his income was, there was no book of any importance in history or biography and the like that was not bought.

Patrick Nicholson, *Vision and Indecision.*

Father had spent all his spare time sitting in the galleries of the House of Commons when he was attending Normal School in Ottawa in 1890-91, and he had many stories of Macdonald and Laurier and the other political giants of those days.

Patrick Nicholson, *Vision and Indecision.*

[On his mother]
She has a very strong personality.

March 29, 1958, *Maclean's.*

I am not going to say that I was much of a teacher myself because my career as one did not last very long. . . . I did not intend to mention this, but the fact was that my clock was fast. During the time I should have been in school I was out shooting gophers. The inspector, the late Dr. Magee, came along and indicated that gopher shooting was not a part of the curriculum and at the termination of the short term my permit was not renewed.

May 22, 1950, House of Commons.

T.C. Davis seems to think that the fact I was once a Liberal is
an offence. Well, as I get older I see the indiscretions of my
youth.

October 15, 1925, *Prince Albert Herald.*

There was no member of my family who was a lawyer. I never
deviated from that course from the time I was eight or nine
years of age. . . . The course was determined for me as a young-
ster, undeviating and unchanging to the destination. . . . It was
all determined for me. I determined myself that that was the
thing I was going to do—and I determined that because of my
being of mixed racial origin.

March 29, 1958, *Maclean's.*

[Of his early days as a lawyer]
No man, however poor, was refused.

September 2, 1967, *Star Weekly.*

After the jury is selected, I focus attention on one person. I
have a little chat with him—not exhortation or verbal fireworks,
but I attempt to speak to him in terms of reasonableness. My
guiding principle is this: cross-examination does not consist of
being cross.

April, 1960, *Liberty.*

I raise no defence *ad hoc* for the profession of law; for all
through the years, from Shakespeare down, from the days of
Jack Cade, it has been the popular thing to excoriate this profession. It needs no defence from outside, but sometimes I
think it needs defence from the inside. Too many of our profession are prone to say of those who undertake—often without
fee—the maintenance of freedom, the assurance of the rights
of the individual, the protection of the weak against the strong,
because these things take place in the criminal courts, that they
do not occupy the same position as those who go into an office
and take up an equally honourable branch of the law.

June 9, 1948, House of Commons.

During my last election campaign in 1940 I had a murder case that took up two of five precious campaign weeks, but in spite of that, or perhaps because of that, I won the election and also got an acquittal for my client.

June 6, 1942, Toronto. *Montreal Standard.*

If there was a proper case, I'd go along with it.

B.T. Richardson, *Canada and Mr. Diefenbaker.*

I have appeared for the defence in several hundreds of cases. I have never had a client who repeated, but in every case where I have acted and the person has been convicted I have taken a personal interest in him when he has come out of jail. . . . I am proud of the fact that I have never had a repeater.

June 7, 1955, House of Commons.

No man can achieve greatness without a wife with the capacity to understand and at the same time be critical in the best sense of the word.

July 30, 1964, House of Commons.

[On his 30th anniversary in Parliament]
On an occasion like this, filled with emotion, I do want to say that one's happiness is greatly increased by having a wife to support and to counsel one. I am not passing that on to the Prime Minister by way of a suggestion, but I say to him that if he would follow my advice in that connection he would be amazed at the transition that would take place.

March 25, 1970, House of Commons.

[On Edna Brower, his first wife]
Isn't Edna wonderful? Wonderful, wonderful. She has got everything that I lack, everything.

Patrick Nicholson, *Vision and Indecision.*

I am constrained, although she would not want me to do so
and will upbraid me for it, to mention my wife, Olive. No man
could have had a better helpmate or a more devoted partner.
June 14, 1962, Television broadcast.

You know, no matter what they say about her [Olive], it will
always be an understatement.
Peter Newman, *Renegade in Power.*

I live each day for itself.
March 29, 1958, *Maclean's.*

I am in bed every night at eleven. I cut off all events of the day.
I never nurse recriminations and I sleep whenever I want to
sleep. I happened to wake up at three o'clock this morning so
I read *The History of State Trials in the United Kingdom.* I can
read three hundred pages an hour.
September 18, 1964, Ottawa.

I just like to work—that's all.
March 29, 1958, *Maclean's.*

Fishing is the only time you can forget everything.
Thomas Van Dusen, *The Chief.*

When I meet a familiar face, I run down the alphabet until my
mind clicks at his initials. I'll talk to him at first of inconse-
quential things to give me time for this mental card-indexing.
Then, when I've reached the letter of the alphabet that coin-
cides with his name, I'll speak his name aloud. If I meet you
five years from now, I'm sure my alphabet run-through system
will work for me.
April, 1960, *Liberty.*

I wish I could be like Elmer [his brother], because everybody
loves him.

Thomas Van Dusen, *The Chief.*

I am asked—and I am speaking to young Canada now—are there
any rewards in public life? There are—not monetary but there
is a tremendous satisfaction in being able to say, "I tried, I
stood."

September, 1967, speech to PC leadership convention.

That participation in public life is a sacrifice is a truism. My
father, who was a teacher, impressed upon the students he
taught the need for participation in public service. Indeed, long
since gone, I think of him in that little school house in East
York where there were 28 students, pupils in all grades. Out of
that number of 28 came four members of the House of Commons. We sat here in 1940; Joe Harris, Robert McGregor,
George Tustin and myself. That was the atmosphere in which
I was raised: the atmosphere of the public service which it was
necessary for men and women with the necessary qualifications
to give in the interests of others.

   All of us have known occasions when we could have left
public life and been better off financially than we are today. I
had that opportunity in large measure in 1942, when had I left
public life and entered one of the great law firms of this country
I would not be in the same financial position today. But I
wanted to be in public life; you do not try five times before
you succeed without having the desire. As I look back over the
years I can say that whatever the vicissitudes of public life,
however great the difficulties of being elected, if I had my life
to live over again, with on the one hand the remuneration which
might have been available and on the other hand the life I have
lived in public service, I would have no reason to change the
ambition that was mine to become a member of the House of
Commons.

July 29, 1963, House of Commons.

You know, when I have finished my long years of public service, I will get a pension of $2,900 a year. Think of that.

John Robert Colombo.

No one can keep from growing old. But I want to tell you this: that if there is anyone here who wants to race me a mile, I'll take him on.

John Robert Colombo.

We westerners realize that even if there is snow on the roof, that does not imply that the fire has gone out of the furnace.

March 25, 1970, House of Commons.

I haven't kept a diary, and there are a lot of things I want to set down. I also want to write a history of Western Canada. I know something about it, and I think I could write a good one. I could easily find plenty to do.

September 15, 1961, *Time*.

I've lived history. I've made history, and I know I'll have my place in history. That's not egoism.

January, 1973, *Maclean's*.

Why do I continue in public life? I still have work to do for Canada. So much to do. So little time to do it.

Fall, 1972, Prince Albert. *Maclean's*, January 1973.

3 "I've always been a House of Commons man."
DIEFENBAKER ON PARLIAMENT

I have loved Parliament.

Dalton Camp, *Gentlemen, Players and Politicians.*

During our day, Parliament was alive—it lived!

January 2, 1973, *Toronto Star.*

Governments propose, and oppositions dispose.

November 2, 1962, House of Commons.

What are the functions of the House of Commons? In order to criticize one must know what the functions are. The most important function is to control the finance of a country; to assure that money shall not be expended that has not been voted; that a full examination be made of all expenditures. The second is the expressive function, the expression of the minds of the people on all matters that come before parliament. The third is the informing function; and the fourth is to legislate.

October 9, 1964, House of Commons.

Parliament is more than procedure—it is the custodian of the nation's freedom.

September 22, 1949, House of Commons.

Parliament is a place where gentlemen meet and what passed between them is not made public.

January 2, 1973, *Toronto Star.*

The business of the country is carried out not by parliament
but by the administrative machinery of the government whether
parliament is sitting or not. But parliament's responsibility and
job is to give careful consideration to policy and the measures
proposed to implement such policy. This it does by time-consum-
ing efforts and processes. It scrutinizes; it questions; it explains;
it criticizes. In other words, it talks.

October 9, 1964, House of Commons.

I would remind you of all the discoveries made in medicine,
science, sociology, and economics that must be translated in
the House of Commons through legislation, before they can be
put to use and work for the public good. Every advance in
human welfare that is achieved must come through this translation, by the parliamentarian.

March 26, 1960. Peter Newman, *Renegade in Power.*

That is freedom of speech—the opportunity to express one's
view in parliament.

January 30, 1942, House of Commons.

The House of Commons is a place where you may disagree, but
you form for those who sit opposite a deep sense of appreciation of their devotion to their country, so long as they speak in
sincerity and truth. And that, I think, is one of the essential
elements.

Peter Gzowski's Book About This Country in the Morning.

Lose morale and you court disaster. Who is the custodian of our
morale? The responsibility rests upon parliament.

January 30, 1942, House of Commons.

[New Members] do one of two things—they grow, or they swell.

November 7, 1974, *Globe and Mail.*

To the young members [of parliament] who have just come I would say that for the first six months after you are here you will wonder how you got here. Then after that you will wonder how the rest of the members ever got here.

September 18, 1968, House of Commons.

The people as a whole should be provided with information as to what is happening in the house. The people should be given the story of parliament as it is. There is nothing more distressing to a new member of parliament, or even a backbench member who has spent time preparing a speech, than to find that, having worked on it for days and having made a study of the subject, he does not get any reference in the press. On the other hand, if the same member were to use language which was unparliamentary he would then be assured of publicity.

October 23, 1963, House of Commons.

[Diefenbaker was once asked in the House to withdraw his charge that Walter Gordon had falsified information and misled the public]

Mr. Speaker, Winston Churchill was once asked to withdraw a statement when he spoke of what had taken place in the house, and he said, "If 'terminological inexactitude' is parliamentary I certainly substitute it with the greatest of pleasure."

March 24, 1964, House of Commons.

Strong men have strong opinions. I think one trend in the last 15 or 20 years has been to reduce the standard of debate in parliament by the insistence on the letter of decorum. . . . If we come to the point where every little expression of criticism results in a request for withdrawal, then indeed will parliament cease to maintain the traditions of the days of Sir John A. Macdonald, D'Arcy McGee, Sir Wilfrid Laurier and Blake. They spoke strongly.

July 12, 1955, House of Commons.

These amateur critics of our parliament ought to read the debates of Britain's parliament. Then they'd begin to understand what harshness in debate means. They've formed the idea that parliament is a kind of sewing circle. They don't know anything about parliament. They never will.

September 2, 1967, *Star Weekly*.

Our parliamentary system cannot exist if obvious and outspoken examples of enmity, and declarations of hatred and contempt, occur between members, or when there is a substitution of personal abuse for argument.

February 2, 1949, House of Commons.

Today there are those seated interruptions. We are all guilty of them. It spoils the appearance of *Hansard*. It gives to readers of *Hansard* the idea that, to use a vulgarism, horseplay is indulged in by members from time to time.

April 20, 1964, House of Commons.

Committees of parliament are not very effective. . . . We in Canada have developed over the years the concept that after all a committee, when it is a political committee, is merely a means, either of refusal or to cover up things that are brought before it.

July 1, 1952, House of Commons.

One of the peculiarities of our political system has been the fact that during the years few women have been elected to the House of Commons. I cannot, at the moment, say what the number has been but it has been comparatively few. If we could think of all of them, it would not take long to repeat their names and their contributions.

November 21, 1960, House of Commons.

The best debates we ever had were on Friday nights. It was on Friday nights, when we were unencumbered by some members who found it necessary to be elsewhere, that parliament was really at its best. I say that those were great days in the House of Commons. They are no different today. The level of debate is just as high, or higher, today as it was then, although each generation looks back at the previous one and says how much better it used to be.

October 17, 1963, House of Commons.

The quality of debate in the House is deplorable. You watch today and count how many read from prepared texts.

May 29, 1971, *Canadian.*

At least I deliver my speeches without reading them.

June 30, 1947, House of Commons.

Some hon. members will recall that in 1912 a very famous member from the city of Montreal spoke for 11½ hours. Then he said, "Mr. Speaker, I am coming to the essence of what I want to place before this house." Those were the happy days.

August 4, 1958, House of Commons.

I have always been a House of Commons man.

June 4, 1964, House of Commons.

One of the major reasons the British parliament has been so effective is that there are no desks before the members of that house that permit of an extensiveness in extemporaneousness aided and abetted by manifold documents on a desk. When a speaker has to bend every now and then in order to remove books and papers from under the seat upon which he is sitting prior to his rising to take part in the debate he is less inclined to have copious reference to voluminous documents.

August 4, 1958, House of Commons.

The removal of the desks would improve the quality of debate in the House of Commons and parliament beyond the imagination of any of us.

July 12, 1955, House of Commons.

Our privileges are fewer than those of members of the British parliament. When approaching parliamentary buildings they have the right over approaching traffic, and are thereby preserved from potential injury. We do not have that here.

January 15, 1953, House of Commons.

I love parliament. When a few power-hungry men decide they are not going to allow it to act, it is something for the people to consider.

March 7, 1963, Guelph, Ontario.

As a result of closure, this institution has been emasculated—it is a eunuch.

March 6, 1973, House of Commons.

As to those who say members of parliament do not work, I should like them to come to Ottawa and see the industry that is displayed by members of this house both inside and outside the house. . . . Too many people believe, and it is not good for public morale, that parliament is stagnant in its enterprise, sterile in its ideas, and complacent when action is demanded.

February 22, 1943, House of Commons.

Mr. Diefenbaker: One of the most serious things about parliament today is the absenteeism—and it has grown and grown with the years. You could get away, as a House, with absenteeism when we were getting $4,000 or $6,000 a year; but when

we are getting $18,000, and $6,000 free of income tax, there
is no justification for continued absence from this chamber.
. . . One of the interesting things as one reads history is to read
the rules of parliament in 1792 when Upper and Lower Canada
joined together under the Constitutional Act. Those rules of
debate were much the same as the rules of debate today, with
one exception. In effect the rule was that no Member should
absent himself without cause, and when the speaker noted his
absence he should forthwith have him brought to the house by
the sheriff.

Some Hon. Members: Oh, oh.

Mr. Diefenbaker: I am not advocating that by any means; the
sheriffs would be too busy.

Some Hon. Members: Hear, Hear.

May 20, 1965, House of Commons.

We would have no more absenteeism in the house after the first
showing of the television across Canada. A daily general survey
of the house by a television camera would do that which nothing
else can possibly achieve.

November 15, 1968, House of Commons.

[On pay raises for members of parliament]
Legislation such as this endangers the institution of parliament,
and places democracy in our country in a position where we,
in parliament, may well be pricing regard for parliament out of
the free market of public opinion.

February 19, 1954, House of Commons.

Many here do not appear to realize that public opinion has
been aroused as I have never known it to be aroused before. I
am speaking becuase I am concerned. In the United Kingdom
parliaments have been called various names. One such parliament was called "Breeches Parliament," and another the "Do

Nothing Parliament." I only hope that this parliament, because of what is taking place, will not be known in history as the "Golden Fleece Parliament."
April 30, 1975, House of Commons.

The period for questions is mainly given to questions, not answers.
November 15, 1968, House of Commons.

Parliament has a soul. Some theorists have always wanted to make it a corporation, with the prime minister as the managing director holding control over a majority of the stock, and with the rest of the shareholders being dominated because of that fact. It is of interest that at this very time when the government, under the leadership of the Prime Minister [Trudeau] and with the assistance of his Man Friday, the hon. member for Rosedale [Donald MacDonald], is trying to crucify parliament, in the U.S.S.R. the intellectuals are doing everything they can to end the concentration of power in the hands of the few to the detriment of the many.
December 13, 1968, House of Commons.

Under the present Prime Minister parliament has been compared to a cemetery operated by its own occupants.
February 17, 1970, House of Commons.

The matter of Senate reform has been a continuing subject of discussion throughout the years, something like the weather.
April 26, 1965, House of Commons.

[Diefenbaker usually referred to the Senate as]
The other place whence no one returns.

It is interesting that an appointment to that body [the Senate] seems to be a tremendous encouragement to longevity.
April 26, 1965, House of Commons.

The Prime Minister is giving a sop to the opposition. If any old Tories in the other place die, he will appoint Tories in their place. That is reform.

October 3, 1974, House of Commons.

I recall very well the election of 1925 when the then Prime Minister, Right Hon. W. L. Mackenzie King, stated that reform of the Senate was a first and foremost course of action needed to assure democracy in this country. He said the same thing in 1926. I recall so well the promises of that day. He said he was going to substitute live Grits for dead Tories in the Senate. Some of those appointed were only half qualified on the basis of Mr. King's description.

April 26, 1965, House of Commons.

[His twenty-fifth anniversary in the House]
The Prime Minister today epitomized the finest traditions of parliament when he added the query, what would the House of Commons be without me. I was reminded of an occasion when that question was asked by a former prime minister, Right Hon. Arthur Meighen, some years after he had been in the House of Commons but before he went to the Senate. He had met with that great wit of parliament S.W. Jacobs, K.C., in Toronto, and asked him, "What is it like in parliament without me?", to which Mr. Jacobs replied, "It is like Hades would be without Satan."

March 26, 1965, House of Commons.

If I should ever leave here, I wouldn't come back. I couldn't come back and just watch from the gallery.

September 2, 1967, Star Weekly.

4 "A prisoner of success."
DIEFENBAKER IN POWER

I don't say everything we did was right. We made mistakes.
June 1, 1962, Kirkland Lake, Ontario.

One prime minister was once asked what his idea of leadership was, and he said that if you compare the electorate to sheep and there are two gates in the corral and you want them to go out one gate but they do not go that way but go through the other gate, you get ahead of them because you are their leader.
January 30, 1973, House of Commons.

It is so strange that such a great honour should come to a small man like me.
June 17, 1957. Pierre Sevigny, *This Game of Politics.*

He who would be chief among you must first be servant of them all.
June, 1962. *Time,* June 8, 1962.

The first responsibility of a prime minister or of the leader of a national party is not to allow himself to be insulated from reality. . . . There is a tendency, not in a sycophantic way, but in a natural way, to tell a person in a position of leadership what is expected will please him. Once if ever that occurs the decisions arrived at will not be based on a realistic appreciation of public opinion.
March 29, 1958, *Maclean's.*

In this job you become a prisoner of success, and it's difficult to know when to stop.
September 15, 1961, *Time.*

Why, it's almost like the night after Waterloo.

The night of the 1957 election upset. Peter Newman, *Renegade in Power.*

For an average Canadian, being chosen as leader of a nation gives one a feeling impossible to describe. You feel a sense of loneliness.

The night of the 1958 election. Peter Newman, *Renegade in Power.*

Once one becomes Prime Minister, all social relationships end.

Patrick Nicholson, *Vision and Indecision.*

The prime minister has all the responsibilities and does all the joe-jobs. I cut down on social functions. No prime minister can carry out his responsibilities when he's going to dinner every night. Dinners are not a substitute for statesmanship.

September 2, 1967, *Star Weekly.*

You know, it's an awesome responsibility to have to ask yourself each day—What will Khruschev do?

March 16, 1963, St. John's, Newfoundland.

Oh, it's not easy for us—the Macmillans, the Kennedys, the Adenauers, and the De Gaulles. . .

June 15, 1962, *Time.*

[At the 1956 leadership convention Diefenbaker was asked to assess his chances]
Well, Don Fleming has been assured that 60% of the delegates will vote for him, and Davie Fulton claims that he has been promised the support of at least 51%; so that leaves a comfortable margin of backing for me!

Patrick Nicholson, *Vision and Indecision.*

In my opinion, nobody, including me, in the future history of Canada, will ever be able to duplicate 1958.

June 8, 1962, *Time.*

I would never have been Prime Minister if the Gallup poll were right.

February 25, 1970, *Toronto Star.*

There is no economic emergency in Canada. There are difficulties.

November 17, 1960, House of Commons.

As long as I am prime minister of this country, I am not going to blame anyone for unemployment.

February 18, 1958, television broadcast.

We recognize the principle that public money should be used to relieve distress on the basis of need, and any scheme which gives no help, or very little, to those who are most in need, is socially indefensible.

March 4, 1960, House of Commons.

[After the forced resignation of James Coyne, Governor of the Bank of Canada]
I have never answered personal attacks. I do not intend to start on this occasion. I do say, however, that whatever the feelings of some Canadians may have been at the beginning of this debate, the last two epistles sent out from the ivory tower, irresponsible and intemperate, sent out on the letterheads and in envelopes belonging to the Bank of Canada and delivered by a personal messenger of the bank, make one wonder. Sir, these letters reveal an attitude which, if accepted by the government, would result in two sovereignties in Canada, the government of Canada and the governor of the Bank of Canada; but not in that order. They would set up a rival government.

July 7, 1961, House of Commons.

Are we going to stop the progress that is taking place, the expansion and the development, by having an election now? I do not mind elections.

October 2, 1962, House of Commons.

I remember that in 1962, during the election of that year, the Minister Without Portfolio [Walter Gordon] and other members of the government were not averse to receiving assistance from the United States. There was assistance in the way of manpower and also the expectation of financial assistance in order to defeat the government. I had the honour to lead because we dared to take a stand on nuclear weapons contrary to the wishes of the United States administration.

March 21, 1967, House of Commons.

As Prime Minister I occupy a house on Sussex Street. That is where I shall be when and if war should come. That is where I shall stay and we have there now a basement shelter identical with the one we have asked Canadians to put in their own homes.

October 6, 1961, *Time*.

We have spent billions of dollars on defence since World War II. Much of what has been spent might be considered by some to have been wasted, but if it had not been for the defences we built up, and those associated with us, our freedom might long since have disappeared. . . . It was not a mistake to take measures to ensure the necessary security, on the basis of the information we had then, even though in light of subsequent events some of the things that were done had been proven, as with every country, to be unnecessary.

January 25, 1963, House of Commons.

We undertook to equip our squadrons assigned to NATO for a strike reconnaissance role, which role would include the mission of delivering nuclear weapons. No one was under any misunderstanding in that connection.

January 25, 1963, House of Commons.

We don't intend to use Canada as a dumping ground for nuclear warheads.

March 4, 1963, Winnipeg.

They say we had a commitment to take nuclear weapons. We did not undertake at any time such a commitment.

March 20, 1963, Edmonton.

Some people talk about courage. Well, we took a stand in reference to the "Arrow." No one wanted to take that stand. . . . As I look back on it, I think it was one of the decisions that was right. Here was an instrument beautiful in appearance, powerful, a tribute to Canadian production. . . . This instrument that was otherwise beautiful, magnificent in its concept, would have contributed little, in the changing order of things, to our national defence.

January 25, 1963, House of Commons.

[After the cancellation of the Avro Arrow contract]
There is no purpose in manufacturing horse collars when horses no longer exist.

March 3, 1959, House of Commons.

They talk about commitments. My friends, this Government has never failed in carrying out any commitment it made.

February 19, 1963, Toronto.

I remember so well, when we said that arrangements were being made to guarantee the sale of wheat to China, that members of the Liberal party—and those members do not sit opposite any more, they are gone—got up and said that it was ridiculous. At that time the President of the United States said, "You are not going to sell wheat to communist China." That is what he told me. . . . Someone suggested that we had taken a tremendous chance. My experience over the years in the ordinary affairs of business and law convinced me that when a Chinese gave his word, he kept it.

June 7, 1967, House of Commons.

[On devaluation of the Canadian dollar]
My brother was in New York the day after we did it. He was told three times what a marvelous thing this would be for the tourist trade.

May 25, 1962, *Time*.

Did you ever know of anyone to whom something has been given who did not want more? That is human nature. When the opposition was in power, the provinces said they were not getting enough. We increased the amount, two, three, four times, five times. And, naturally, they said: Don't we get more than this?

September 27, 1961, House of Commons.

The Prime Minister and the premiers are meeting. I hope they will be able to achieve the repatriation of the constitution. We almost succeeded and would have done so but for one or two comparatively minor matters to which objection was taken by the province of Quebec and, even more so, by the province of Saskatchewan when that province was under a socialist government.

September 1, 1964, House of Commons.

[At a cabinet meeting, during the cabinet revolt of 1963]
Those who are with me, stand up! Those against me, remain seated.

Patrick Nicholson, *Vision and Indecision*.

I've got all my enemies in the cabinet where I can keep an eye
on them.

Attributed to Diefenbaker. March 14, 1959, *Maclean's*.

My wife came to tell me that Hees and Sevigny had arrived and
wanted to see me. So I put on some clothes and went down-
stairs. "It's a wonderful morning, Prime Minister," Hees greet-
ed me, then muttered something about an obvious disagreement.
"That's my resignation," he added abruptly, handing me an
envelope. "My honour demands that I resign too," said Sevigny,
also handing over an envelope. I was amazed, I thought we were
all together. But of course it was all part of a plot, as I learned
afterwards. These two resignations were expected to force me
to resign and, if I did not, there were to be two more resignations in the afternoon. But they never came.

Patrick Nicholson, *Vision and Indecision*.

[In 1966 Diefenbaker found himself on the defensive once
again over his treatment of the Munsinger affair]
The President of the Privy Council [Guy Favreau] some days
ago told me of the hon. members sitting on this side of the
house that if we pressed the Spencer case there would be a
revelation relating to what took place during my administration. The Minister of Justice [Lucien Cardin] looked over at
me and said, in effect, "We will fix you."

March 7, 1966, House of Commons.

I called in the Minister [Pierre Sevigny]. I made it very clear to
him that I would not stand for a continuation of any relationship. He was a man with a distinguished war record. It ended
there. There was no continuation of the relationship.

There has been no suggestion that at any time she directly
or indirectly engaged in espionage.

What else could I do? I exercised the discretion of a prime
minister, the responsibility of a prime minister, which is not
subject to review by any commission.

May 25, 1966, television broadcast.

I unequivocally repeat that there never was a question of security in connection with this matter.
May 20, 1966, *Time.*

It is not for me, after almost 26 years in this chamber, to apologize for any action taken during the period I was Prime Minister or at any other time.
March 14, 1966, House of Commons.

I do not say that everything I did was right, but what I do say, Mr. Speaker, is that what I did was honest.
March 24, 1966, House of Commons.

Criticism is essential in the democratic process, but the organized deluge of defamation and adjectival abuse that has been heaped on the Government of this country and myself as leader has never been equalled in the history of Canada.
October 12, 1962, *Time.*

How can we organize these things if they hold up everything?
February 5, 1963, House of Commons.

We won the by-elections but when we came to the general elections we were not so successful.
January 22, 1962, House of Commons.

When we started out there was a feeling we were on our way out. . . . Now there is a realization, except on the part of a few deluded persons, that we are on our way in.
April 4, 1963, Hamilton.

No, I am not a showman. A man in politics must do one thing. He must be himself. Nor am I ashamed of being called a politician, a person engaged in the science of politics. I like quoting President Harry Truman's definition of a statesman. "A statesman is a politician who is dead."
April, 1960, *Liberty.*

My friends, you say, "Give 'em hell, John!" I never do that. I
tell the truth and it sounds like hell. It simply sounds that way
to the Grits.
March 13, 1963, Moncton, N.B.

Without an Opposition, it is not too much to say, the parliamentary system of government would fail in its primary task
of protecting the rights of individuals and minorities, and of
ensuring freedom and democracy.
Those Things We Treasure.

Tierney once said that the duty of an opposition is to propose
nothing, to oppose everything and to turn out the government
at the next election. I agree with the last of Tierney's defini-
tions.
March 24, 1953, House of Commons.

Autocracy, tyranny, dictatorship, are shadows that ever stand
in the wings of even the freest of parliaments. In the absence
of a strong Opposition, a cabinet with a commanding position
in the House could and would rule without regard to individual
and minority rights.
Those Things We Treasure.

Oppositions cleanse and purify those in office and we in the
opposition are in fact the "detergents of democracy."
November 24, 1964, House of Commons.

The Opposition finds fault; it suggests amendments; it asks
questions and elicits information; it arouses, educates and
moulds public opinion by voice and vote. It must scrutinize

every action by the Government; and in doing so prevent the
short-cuts through democratic procedure that Governments like
to make. . . . Parliament will only remain the guardian of freedom and our free institutions so long as His Majesty's Loyal
Opposition is fully responsible and effective in the discharge of
its functions.

Patrick Nicholson, *Vision and Indecision.*

I've enjoyed my two periods as leader of the Opposition. It's
a much freer life than Prime Minister and you have an almost
equal scope of making a contribution.

September 18, 1964, Ottawa.

Our paramount consideration as members of the opposition
must be to refrain from obstructive criticism and fearlessly to
offer constructive criticism.

June 10, 1941, House of Commons.

The duty of the Opposition is to turn out the government.

March 13, 1964, Ottawa. Peter Newman, *The Distemper of Our Time.*

[On the Mackenzie King government]
We who are on this side of the house are now faced by a government which, in its greed for power, and at the expense of the
House of Commons, has gone farther than any other government in Canada ever dreamed of going in a time of war or
peace, and almost as far, indeed if not actually as far, as the
socialist government in Great Britain has gone.

December 11, 1947, House of Commons.

[Diefenbaker's debut as Leader of the Opposition]
As the Prime Minister [Louis St. Laurent] showed such an
intimate knowledge of the responsibilities of an Opposition, I
hope the opportunity will come to him and to Canada to dis-
play that knowledge.

January 17, 1957, House of Commons.

If you send this [the St. Laurent] Government back to office,
don't ask Her Majesty's Loyal Opposition to stand up for your
rights. For you no longer will have any rights.

1957 election campaign, Hanover, Ontario. Peter Newman, *Renegade in
Power.*

When we came into office in 1957, not one member of our
Cabinet had ever seen the Cabinet room. We had been out of
office so long that we had almost an exemplification of eternity.

September, 1967, PC leadership convention.

While wars on poverty are essential, they will be won when we
raise economic standards in our nation, when the humblest in
the land is not forgotten but has a voice in parliament. Fifty
million dollars is going to the big manufacturers of automobiles
and parts. But when anybody suggested that $75 was too little
for the old age pensioners, the government said wait. Fifty
million dollars for the manufacturers but no addition for the
old age pensioners.

April 6, 1965, House of Commons.

[On old age pensions]
No matter what attitude the government adopts, what is being
done here is an application of the means test. The government
tries to dignify it by calling it another name, but a rose by any
other name is just as sweet and a thorn by any other name is
just as Sharp.

December 15, 1966, House of Commons.

The means test is the meanest test of all becuase it is applied to
the average person across the country and places everyone in a
position of mental or physical subservience.

July 7, 1972, House of Commons.

It was on a night such as this that Rivard went out to water the
rink. . . .

A favorite riposte throughout the 1965 election campaign.

There are two courses open when wrong doing is encountered
in government. It can be dealt with swiftly and effectively, or
it can be condoned. You cannot meet widespread wrongdoing
by issuing codes of ethics. Well, the Prime Minister's attitude
is that of the three monkeys: see no evil, speak no evil, and if
you hear any evil, forget it.

October 7, 1965, television broadcast.

There are two flags, two pension schemes, and two types of
law—one for us and the other for the Bananas and the Mananas
and the rest of that menagerie.

1965 election campaign. *Maclean's,* January 1, 1966.

I never will ascribe to this government such wrongdoing as mere
stupidity will explain.

November 24, 1966, House of Commons.

The Liberal party used to stand for freedom for the individual.
That was prior to 1940. Since then its members have followed
another course. Since then they have developed the philosophy
that, "After all, it does not really matter so long as it is effi-
cient."

December 19, 1966, House of Commons.

The fact is that the [Trudeau] government has no legislation
ready to go ahead with. It may have legislation on the Criminal
Code; it can prepare legislation in order to aid abortion and
multiply homosexuality. It has that legislation ready.

December 13, 1968, House of Commons.

I have never in 30 years seen Parliament treated with the
egregious contempt that is being shown to Parliament by the
present administration.

February 17, 1970, House of Commons.

Where, where is the nation going?
January 11, 1973, House of Commons.

I never once regarded a defeat as a termination. I have been
beaten often, but I have never been spiritually vanquished. The
day after a defeat at the polls, I was always back at work. I
never felt hurt or whipped.
April, 1960, *Liberty.*

[In Cabinet Council, after the 1962 election which returned
the Conservatives to power as a minority government]
I didn't ask for this job, and I don't want it. If I'm no longer
wanted, I'll go.
Patrick Nicholson, *Vision and Indecision.*

There is not going to be another minority government when I
look into the faces of my fellow Canadians.
March 8, 1963, Belleville, Ontario.

They think I'm fighting too hard. I don't know any other way
to fight.
1964. Thomas Van Dusen, *The Chief.*

I have been maligned. I have been condemned. No one since
the days of Macdonald has gone through the like. . . . They say
they want to remove me. . . . I have been told in the last few
days that if I remain as leader of the Conservative Party, support for the Party by certain interests will end. My friends, they
believe that they will succeed in this way. I will follow the will
of the people. Will it be the will of the people or those that are
all powerful?
February 19, 1965, television broadcast.

They say they want to remove me. Well, it is not ambition that
keeps me, it is a desire to serve.
February 19, 1965, television broadcast.

[Four days before the 1965 election]
You've lavished me with everything, since my humblest of
beginnings. You raised me to the responsibilities of leadership,
you gave me everything, and in the service of my country I have
given the full span of man's normal years. I'd like you to think,
I hope you will believe, that whatever my shortcomings, these
years were not unworthy.
November 4, 1965, Edmonton. *Maclean's*, January 1, 1966.

There is nothing as lonely as the leadership of a national party.
If things go right, others get the credit. If things go wrong, the
leader takes it—excoriated, condemned. I stood because I knew
that sooner or later the people would realize our policies were
right.
November 5, 1965, Regina.

You have always tried to tie somebody to the stake for your
responsibility. As I listened to the minister [Mitchell Sharp]
the other night I must say that his description of me, by infer-
ence, could only be applied to His Satanic Majesty. I am to
blame for almost everything. No matter what this government
does not do, it is the Leader of the Opposition who is to blame.
When I think of the three or four years of calumny that has
been heaped on me, when I think of the colouring books, the
truth squads, the pigeons and all those other instruments,
mental offspring of some of the members now sitting on the
front bench, I realize that they have tried everything. Those in
the press who support them have joined in. They pictured me
as suffering from an incurable disease. I have an incurable disease and it is this, the desire to do something for Canada.
September 9, 1966, House of Commons.

[At the annual Conservative meeting of 1966, after Dalton
Camp was elected president]
Fight on, my men, I am wounded but I am not slain. I'll lay
me down and rest awhile and then I'll rise again.
November 16, 1966.

They thought Winston Churchill wouldn't win again. They thought he was too old. . .

September 2, 1967, *Star Weekly.*

[Before the Conservative leadership convention of 1967] They'll never vote for a man of 72.

Thomas Van Dusen, *The Chief.*

My course has come to an end, and I have fought your battles, and you have given that loyalty that led us to more victories than this party has had since the days of Macdonald. . . . Now, taking my retirement, I say this to you, with the deepest of feeling: my country; I have nothing to withdraw in my desire to see Canada one country, one nation—my country and your country. . . . From the bottom of my heart, I thank you for having given me this opportunity to serve in my day and generation.

Closing speech to the 1967 PC leadership convention.

I've always been accessible. Unlike some people. If I hadn't been *so* accessible to some people, I wouldn't be where I am now.

May 29, 1971, *Canadian.*

Naturally, there are things you'd change if you had that valuable aid, hindsight. But one always has the satisfaction of knowing that those who are the most bitterly attacked, often, in the light of history, assume different proportions.

September 2, 1967, *Star Weekly.*

I have sometimes been wrong; I have never been on the side of wrong.

An oft-repeated remark.

They say I've made mistakes, but they've been mistakes of the heart.
April 6, 1963, *Maclean's.*

Law firms want me on their letterhead. And they'd pay me $100,000 a year just to hang around. But that's not the way I want to go out.
May 29, 1971, *Canadian.*

I'll be there when the House meets and I'll still be fighting.
1968 campaign. Thomas Van Dusen, *The Chief.*

6 "Right here in Canada today . . ."
DIEFENBAKER ON DOMESTIC AFFAIRS

"Politics as usual," with its companion, "business as usual," is a dangerous partnership in time of war. Canada today is asking her men to do and to give their all, and they ask us to make our objective victory and not votes. Let us forget our partisanship, which we have shown in the past. All of us have been guilty. Let our party drums cease to rumble, and let not party declarations stymie us from our goal of a total war effort, stultifying the national war effort and stagnating the people's morale and their will to do and their will to serve.

January 30, 1942, House of Commons.

This legislation [the Treachery Act] is designed to render impotent the quislings and those of like mind for the period of the war. To those who say that they do not believe the death penalty should be imposed, let me point out that the law today is that the death penalty shall be imposed upon one who commits treason. Treason may be committed in any number of ways.

July 25, 1940, House of Commons.

It is only right that when a man is truly a conscientious objector his scruples should be considered.

February 24, 1943, House of Commons.

I feel that the members of this house owe it to the women in the armed services of this country to protect their names from calumny which all too frequently is indulged in. . . . All of us have occasion to see the wonderful work that these women are doing in the air force and in the other services, and we as members and as Canadians owe it to them to uphold their good name and to assure those who dare to scandalize them that they will be fittingly punished.

1943, House of Commons.

I point this out, too, to those who say we need a united Canada in this war, that in these casualty lists of the air force will be seen many names of Ukrainians, Scandinavians, and those of German origin who have enlisted from western Canada.
March 29, 1943, House of Commons.

We have got to look after these fellows [returning veterans]. I don't want them to go through what I went through after I returned from overseas in the last war.
May 28, 1942, House of Commons.

People do not want to believe there is going to be atomic bombing of Canada. The thought disturbs our equanimity. We like to look at the situation as though we were protected and insulated by many thousands of miles of sea and a northern ice cap. It is going to require an educational campaign to make the people realize the danger in which we find ourselves.
May 25, 1957, House of Commons.

[On the Soviet announcement of plans to test an atomic bomb] The explosion of such a diabolical device would be a brutal offense against humanity for which there can be no justifiable excuse, either in terms of defense or of simple common sense. No one can deny that continued experimentation of these devices will ultimately lead to a war measured in megadeaths.
October 27, 1961, *Time.*

The aquisition of Newfoundland will take its place, in strategic importance, with the acquisition by the United States of Alaska and Louisiana.
February 8, 1949, House of Commons.

The mail service is totally inexcusable.
July 3, 1952, House of Commons.

Every day in every way we the people of Canada are paying a
tribute to these companies which have taken undue advantage
of the people of Canada.

July 2, 1946, House of Commons.

Businessmen, where are your voices today? In 1911 you
spoke. But today you are silent while things are done which
you know are wrong. You watch this government going along
the road to socialism. Is it that, fearing you will be called cap
in hand to the throne of bureaucracy, you seek to protect
yourselves with your silence? If so, you will only tighten the
bands that still bind you.

February 18, 1948, speech to PC Business Men's Club, Toronto. *Globe
and Mail.*

One of the great criticisms of our system is that it lives by re-
turning profit. Business requires profit. Profit is of prime
importance to the maintenance of our way of life. The profit
system spells our prosperity.

November 14, 1949, House of Commons.

The penalty under the combines legislation is a fine of $10,000,
a fraction of what the illicit gains may be to those who by design evade the law and exploit the country. . . . It is robbery.
Potential profits great; potential penalty picayune.

October 17, 1951, House of Commons.

We are at a point where more and more the procedure of
criminal law must be appealed to in order to place great and
powerful corporations in a position where they cannot detri-
mentally affect the health, the comfort or the welfare of the
people as a whole.

February 12, 1954, House of Commons.

I believe that we have imposed on rail transportation too much legislation and too many rules. Some of those rules must be revised but that does not mean that we should give to those kindly, gentle and philanthropic boards of directors of the great railway companies the power to make Canadians pay through the nose where there is no competition to keep freight rates down.

September 8, 1966, House of Commons.

Government only makes money in business if it has a monopoly, such as the liquor business. Government can always make a success of the liquor business. As long as there is water in the rivers, there will be a profit. You can't lose.

March 12, 1958, Nanaimo, B.C.

I am one of those who believe that the price controls effective in time of war because of the mobilization of all the people in the state would be less than successful in times of a reasonably free economy.

August 21, 1958, House of Commons.

[On government spending]
A Trojan horse has found its way into the camp of the people of Canada: it consists of a desire to overexpend and a refusal to control, regardless of the demands in all parts of this country for curtailment. Over and over again, the attitude has been, spend, spend, spend!

July 10, 1946, House of Commons.

When Canadians are being taxed at the highest level in Canadian history, surely they have a right to ask that the attitude of the government will not be that of the Minister of Trade and Commerce [C.D. Howe] —"What is a million, anyhow?"

January 15, 1953, House of Commons.

Too much and too many of the moneys extorted and squeezed from the Canadian people are being wasted by the parasites of extravagance.

March 6, 1953, House of Commons.

The view of the ivory tower boys seems to be that if you spend your money it makes inflation, but if the government takes it from you and spends it, no harm is done.

April 25, 1957, Toronto.

The government is its own major contribution to inflation in this country.

April 11, 1957, House of Commons.

I intend to make some references which are based on evidence contained in the report of the Auditor General. That report is a lexicon of laxity and wild expenditure. Never since the horses were on the payroll has there been such a condemnation of a government.

February 2, 1966, House of Commons.

I could give no better description of this budget than to use the words of Abraham Lincoln when, in 1858, he described a budget by saying it "was as thin as the homeopathic soup that was made by boiling the shadow of a pigeon that had starved to death."

March 17, 1970, House of Commons.

I'm disturbed because the doctors tell me I'm as sound as a dollar.

April 25, 1975, Ottawa.

We should arrive at a plan in this parliament, whether by way of the compulsory vote or otherwise, whereby our people will be required to discharge their responsibilities.

June 15, 1948, House of Commons.

On one occasion during the course of a meeting in my constituency, a question was raised with regard to compulsory voting.
Among those present was an elderly gentleman who made his
contribution. . . . He said that he had given consideration to an
alternative which would do away with the necessity of compulsory voting but would assure that people would indeed
exercise their franchise. This old homesteader's plan was that
no one should have the right to go on the voters' list unless he
registered and, at the same time, paid a fee of $2. At the time
he came to vote, a part of the ballot would consist of a counter-
foil which would entitle the person who had voted to the return of the $2. He said he believed that if his system were
adopted there would be an almost 100% vote in every election.
I had never heard the suggestion before, Mr. Speaker, but it has
merit.

December 14, 1951, House of Commons.

[On electoral redistribution]
We believe that the will of the people should not be thwarted
or diminished by crude efforts, in some cases, or the redrawing
of maps of peculiar shape and form in order to remove those
whose presence in this chamber would be regarded by a government with a large majority as inimical to the quietude of the
soul of that government.

April 9, 1962, House of Commons.

In two different and successive redistributions I found my constituency operated on without anaesthetic by the government
of those days for the political purposes of that government.

April 29, 1966, House of Commons.

Royal commissions are set up for one of two purposes: first,
to secure information upon which a decision may be made or,
secondly, to evade responsibility for the making of any decision.

February 18, 1949, House of Commons.

Royal commissions sit, recommend, and then there is deep discussion and consideration by governments for such a length of time that ultimately the report of the royal commission finds itself resting in the dust of some alcove used for storage purposes.

June 26, 1967, House of Commons.

When we are elected to office, we will set up a royal commission and we will clean up the mess.

October 27, 1965, St. John, N.B.

In the development of a Canadian nationality everything should be done by the government to encourage and develop Canadian literature and drama and art. . . . One of the most trying problems in this country to-day is that having given our young Canadians an opportunity of securing a wide education, when they have finished that education, too often by reason of the greater monetary attractions of the United States the cultural development which they should have left in our country is lost to us.

April 2, 1946, House of Commons.

Last year 73,000 people came to Canada as immigrants, while 31,000 left Canada as emigrants. That shows that there is something wanting, something that has to be done. After all it does not mean very much to have an immigration policy under which two people are brought into our country while one Canadian leaves in the same period.

April 29, 1951, House of Commons.

[On censorship legislation]
It is always difficult for legislation to maintain freedom of speech and at the same time prevent the exercise of licence by those who would destroy morals for monetary benefit.

December 5, 1949, House of Commons.

While these amendments are stern, and wipe out some of the things upon which our heritage and freedom are based, in the administration of criminal law they can be justified only on the ground that obscene and lascivious books, which have no purpose other than that of monetary gain derived from their lewdness and indecency, are available.

December 5, 1949, House of Commons.

In Canada today we have a definite crime wave.

December 12, 1945, House of Commons.

Today we ameliorate or increase punishment more or less in a haphazard and uncertain way. From year to year we follow a system of selective uncertainty.

June 15, 1948, House of Commons.

I am sure all of us who have read Dickens' story about Little Dorritt will realize that, actually, what we are doing in this twentieth century, by imposing imprisonment in default of payment of a fine, is in effect a continuation of that to which Dickens had reference when he dealt with the deplorable situation then prevailing in the prisons.

March 11, 1954, House of Commons.

The stigma of gaol stays with a man throughout his life. No matter what he does he is always faced with that circumstance, that some place, somehow, he served time.

July 3, 1947, House of Commons.

After a man or woman has served a term in a penitentiary and has then lived a life free of crime for a period of 5 to 10 years his or her record should be washed clear. When I was prime minister I received an application for a pardon. I have to be pretty general in referring to it because this man occupies a high position in our country. When he was 19 or 20 he committed

an offence for which he was sent to the penitentiary. The years
went by and now he occupies a position in which he does good
not only for the people of our country but for humanity. I
believe that men in that position deserve to have their records
cleared.

June 26, 1967, House of Commons.

No amount of bail will prevent those who would escape from
getting away if the opportunity offers itself. I can think of
examples which readily occur. I think of Hal Banks who today
sojourns in the salubrious areas of the United States. Convicted
in Canada, sentenced to five years, let out on bail for $25,000,
he finds it much more in tune with his sensitivities to be abroad.

June 16, 1967, House of Commons.

Some wonder why I have such a feeling of concern over the
imposition of the death penalty. I ask those who wonder how
would you feel if you defended a man charged with murder,
who was as innocent as any hon. member in this House at this
very moment, who was convicted; whose appeal was dismissed,
who was executed; and six months later the star witness for
the Crown admitted that he, himself, had committed the
murder and blamed it on the accused? That experience will
never be effaced from my memory.

May 1, 1972, House of Commons.

My great-grandfather saw a boy hanged in Upper Canada for
picking pockets in 1837. I think the boy was seventeen years
of age and everybody gathered for the public execution. There
was a great celebration, and during the ceremonies of the execution four of them had their pockets picked, which just
indicates the argument that the fear of capital punishment will
greatly reduce the number of offences is not completely tenable, if tenable at all.

An argument retold many times.

[The following are excerpted from Diefenbaker's speech on capital punishment, made in the House on April 4, 1966.]

All of us realize the awful problem we face; all of us have reasons for making clear our individual views. Mine, in summary, were expressed many years ago by John Donne when he said, "Any man's death diminishes me because I am involved in mankind."

Some quote Scripture and say it is difficult for a rich man to enter the kingdom of heaven. A cynic would ask whether a rich man, leaving aside the kingdom of heaven, is not virtually secured against a meeting with the hangman on the gallows?

Anyone who says an innocent man cannot go to the gallows is wrong.

The first great abolitionist was William the Conqueror. He was opposed to the death sentence. He said he did not believe in the death sentence and substituted maiming, the removal of arms, legs, eyes and ears. His reasoning was that the trunk must remain alive as a witness of its crimes. We think of Henry VIII and his multiplicity of conjugal murders but do not recall that 72,000 were hanged for stealing during his reign. This did not reduce the number of thefts. Elizabeth, in the name of humanity, said, "I have to bring about a change in the death sentence." There were two varieties of the death sentence in those days. You were either executed on the gibbet by being put in chains and hung up and left until your soul went to its Maker or you went to the scaffold. There you suffocated. Elizabeth said that in the name of humanity a change had to be made and people could not be hung in chains unless strangled beforehand. They said this was necessary. They quoted scripture.

About 150 years ago the theft of five shillings was punishable by death. Many said this punishment was salutary, that it was punitive and above all a deterrent.

The time has passed by when the idea of vengeance any longer has any place in our society.

January 30, 1973, House of Commons.

We have been wasteful and destructive of the great resources we have in our country. In the years ahead, 30 to 40 years from now, water will be more valuable to Canada if we maintain its purity than many of our other resources.

May 5, 1964, House of Commons.

Yes, that's it, the *hippies*. Well, they've found an answer to the age-old problem of living without working. But I don't find them as unattractive . . . no, don't say that . . . I don't find them as *unique* as some people do. They're a manifestation of a passing fad.

February 10, 1968, *Star Weekly*.

7 "A gardener of democracy."
DIEFENBAKER ON EXTERNAL AFFAIRS

If Canada had taken the attitude in 1935 and 1936, and up to
the outbreak of the war, that she takes today; if she had let
the world and the aggressor nations know then what her stand
would be should war come, would the result have been different? That will always remain an enigma of history.

July 9, 1943, House of Commons.

When the atomic bomb fell on Japan on August 8 there was an
end to an era of man's thinking on international affairs, and I
believe an end to man's thinking on life as it had been; for now
all realize more than ever, as the hon. member of Rosetown-
Biggar [M.J. Coldwell] said this afternoon, isolationism no
longer can be the cult of any political party or of any nation.

October 18, 1945, House of Commons.

Although Canada is in the foothills and not at the summit, we
can all be visited with disaster by the storms that gather round
the peaks.

June 13, 1960, *Time*.

. . . Ottawa, the centre of the world to-day on the air routes of
the world and the interpreter of the will of the British people
to the United States of America and also the interpreter of the
United States of America to the people of Britain.

July 9, 1943, House of Commons.

By the accident of geography and history we find ourselves
squarely between the two greatest powers on earth. We have
no fortresses facing either. We want to live at peace with our
northern neighbours, as we have lived so long at peace with
our southern neighbours.

September 26, 1960, speech to the United Nations.

The Commonwealth connection and all it stands for, both practically and traditionally, is one of the glories of our Canadian heritage. It is the outstanding example in all world history of amity among free and independent people. Our Commonwealth has no written constitution. It has neither laws nor by-laws to define the mutual responsibilities of its membership. The only obligations it imposes are those of good sense, good faith, and goodwill. The ties that bind the Commonwealth together are family ties—and what a remarkable family it is!

June 22, 1957, House of Commons.

[On the foundation of the United Nations]
This charter makes for great idealisms. It is, as Anthony Eden said, mankind's last chance.

October 19, 1945, House of Commons.

The United Nations must be supported as never before. Undermining it by criticism that is unfounded will destroy that only agency that can preserve peace.

February 13, 1953, House of Commons.

We in Canada should join the other members of the United Nations in the establishment of a world food bank, whereby reserves would be made available for distribution in those parts of the world that are today facing starvation and whereby surpluses that heretofore have resulted in a major fall in prices would instead be used for the benefit of mankind. Certainly something must be done to encourage agricultural production in this country.

December 17, 1951, House of Commons.

We are not here in this Assembly to win wars of propaganda. We are here to win victories for peace.

September 26, 1960, speech to the United Nations.

The United Nations today is a denuded shadow of what we believed it could be in San Francisco in 1945.
May 1, 1970, House of Commons.

NATO, the Atlantic bastion of freedom against the floodtide of communism.
December 21, 1958, television broadcast.

I know that in this regard Lord Ismay said that NATO is to some rather a lot of harness and not much horse.
April 2, 1952, House of Commons.

I saw the nations working together in San Francisco. I saw there Molotov, often the enigma, but a man who indicated in every way that the desire of his nation was to assure its full contribution to peace.
October 19, 1945, House of Commons.

There exists in Canada a fifth column organized and directed by Russian agents in Canada and in Russia.
June 8, 1948, House of Commons.

Communism is undermining our nation in various places. Ask the mounted police.
April 26, 1949, House of Commons.

One of the greatest allies Stalin has in the world today is inflation. . . . We cannot beat Stalin with a 56-cent dollar.
April 20, 1951, House of Commons.

What is taking place in Korea is not war, but rather the punishment of an international aggressor by the combined conscience of mankind.
June 15, 1951, House of Commons.

When one reads that in some parts of the world a man who has
made the supreme sacrifice in Korea is denied burial in the
cemetery of some democratic country, I wonder whether those
who follow that course realize that what they are doing accen-
tuates the possibility of communism taking over the coloured
races.

April 2, 1952, House of Commons.

The gardeners of democracy have become weary of removing
the weeds of communism. Nations are becoming weary of
tending the vineyard of freedom. France is tax-weary and
Italy has fallen by the way. The United States and Britain are
left alone to fight what will be the greatest fight in British history. If we in Canada are to preserve freedom throughout our
land, we must retain the closest possible co-operation with all
parts of the Commonwealth and with the United States.

March 6, 1952, Toronto.

What communism uses above everything else is the H-weapon,
the weapon of hunger.

March 10, 1952, House of Commons.

The Soviets smile, but at the same time they try to create and
foster discord among the members of the United Nations. Co-
existence is a seductive word. One of their smartest pieces of
propaganda ever developed is the use of that word.

January 20, 1955, House of Commons.

There cannot be friendship and understanding between the
continents if the Western world arrogantly assumes a monopoly
of skill and wisdom or that we must try to make all other peoples conform to our way of thinking.

June, 1958, Toronto. *Saturday Night*, November 22, 1958.

Mr. Khruschev and his comrades in the Kremlin are specialists
in the application of the technique of the carrot and stick, of
alternating smiles and threats. They do not lack a theoretical
foundation for their policies but sometimes it appears they
have adapted to their purposes for international use, the
Pavlovian theory of psychology as practised on dogs. According to this theory the way to break down a dog is to apply
positive and negative stimuli, and in turn to be nice, unkind or
cool, to feed it, forget it, ring bells, flash lights, so that the dog
will go all to pieces in a desperate effort to make head or tail
of what is going on.

1960. B.T. Richardson, *Canada and Mr. Diefenbaker.*

There is no way in which you can fill empty stomachs by the
promises of congressional or parliamentary government.

May 22, 1961, *U.S. News & World Report.*

If the Soviet system is paradise, why is it that the people of
West Berlin do not beset the Brandenburg Gate and beseech
the burgomaster of East Berlin for citizenship?

August 15, 1961, Halifax.

Retreat in Berlin, by the sacrifice of the pledged word, would
mean that the pledged word of the West would be called in
question everywhere in the world with consequences impossible
to calculate for the future of freedom.

September 1961, Winnipeg. *Time,* September 8, 1961.

It is very interesting to read the Communist manifesto. I am
not going into details with regard thereto, but I suggest to Hon.
Members that they read the text of the Soviet Party's draft
programme for the next 20 years. Hitler took 1,000 pages in
"Mein Kampf." Khruschev takes less than 50 pages, and he

places before the world the blueprint of the architect, in which he builds a house for all mankind, with the U.S.S.R. having the only key to the premises.

September 11, 1961, House of Commons.

There will be no second prizes in the next world war.

May 23, 1967, House of Commons.

Why should a powerful nation stoop to deprive its citizens of their religion and of their traditional symbols used in religious observances? What justification can there be in depriving Jews of unleavened bread at the Passover? In recent months Soviet courts have handed down savage punishment to persons convicted of economic crimes. Such treatment seems hardly fitting for a nation which claims a high and steady growth rate in living standards.

April 4, 1962, Montreal.

I recall that some years ago Canada received a gift of a magnificent clock from the U.S.S.R. It was the finest piece of antique artistry that the U.S.S.R. could give us. It was set up in the offices of the Canadian embassy in Moscow. It was not until two years later that it was found to have a bug in it and that everything that was ever said in that room was available to the U.S.S.R. That was bugging of an advanced character.

May 8, 1973, House of Commons.

I frankly state that in 1948 my own party came out in favour of outlawing communism. I was the only one to oppose it. I received a very unusual lack of welcome. The Conservative party was going to sweep Canada with that policy. I said, "You cannot do it. You cannot deny an individual the right to think as he will. The offence is not in being wrong, the offence is in doing wrong. Whenever communism has been outlawed it has

operated underground. When it has come out, it has been
stronger than ever."
October 16, 1970, House of Commons.

China is a country of 600 million people and a population such
as that cannot be ignored. We have in the past had a long and
friendly relationship with the Chinese people. . . . The question
of recognition of the Peking regime is a difficult and complex
one. . . . We felt that recognition would be interpreted in many
parts of the world, among those who have taken a strong stand
against communism and its dangers, as recognition of communism
rather than the application of the legalistic principle. We do not
intend to take any course which will weaken the opposition to
communism.
1958 Commonwealth tour. *Saturday Night,* January 17, 1959.

No international thug should be allowed to shoot its way into
the United Nations.
March 25, 1954, House of Commons.

All over the world, Canada has a black eye. And now what is
the government doing? It has recognized Communist China.
Well, I can just imagine the deluge of communist spies who will
come in here attached to the Chinese embassy when it opens.
October 16, 1970, House of Commons.

Well, and I think this expression is to be ascribed to Mao, for
anyone to suggest that communism and the western world can
coexist side by side is as ridiculous as endeavouring to fry an
iceberg.
October 16, 1970, House of Commons.

Canada has no intention whatsoever of imposing any embargo
on Canadian goods in Cuban trade.
October, 1960, Winnipeg. *Time,* October 31, 1960.

Cuba is a casualty of the internationalization of its original revolution. In this process, the interests of the Cuban people have been subordinated to the interplay of outside forces beyond their control. Civil liberties are curtailed in the name of national security, and arbitrary acts of reprisal have become a substitute for justice. These are manifestations of a dictatorship which is abhorrent to free men everywhere.

April 28, 1961, *Time.*

When my hon. friend spoke this afternoon of the rise of Arab nationalism I thought of the book by Nasser entitled "Egypt's Liberation." That little book of 120 pages or so is the blueprint upon which Nasser has proceeded. He set the course out as clearly as ever did Hitler whose viewpoint in Mein Kampf few regarded seriously until it was too late. . . . He fomented. He aroused. He inspired. That is why, because of this matter of nationalism, the Arab countries cannot be taken for granted.

July 25, 1958, House of Commons.

President Nasser impresses me as a man with tremendous capacity and ability, dedicated to the building of his country. . . . I do not believe that they have in contemplation the launching of any attack against Israel.

November 28, 1963, House of Commons.

This Commonwealth, with five out of six belonging to a coloured race, cannot, dare not, be other than colour blind.

1960 Prime Ministers' conference in London.

[On the admission of South Africa to the Commonwealth] Apartheid has become a world symbol of discrimination. I took the position that if we accepted South Africa unconditionally, the action would be taken as approval, or at least condonation, of racial policies which are abhorred by Canadians as a whole.

March, 1961, House of Commons.

I made it clear that the policy of South Africa was a denial of the principle that human dignity and the worth of the individual, whatever his race and colour, must be respected, and that there could be no doubt as to our views in that connection.

March 1960, House of Commons.

[On the closing of the Canadian embassy in Saigon]
All over Asia, Canada will be pointed at with critical fingers. Canada left. Where was Canada?

April 25, 1975, Ottawa.

Canada has become a joke in the eyes of the world.

September 18, 1970, *Toronto Telegram.*

8 "I never make personal allusions."
DIEFENBAKER ON HIS CONTEMPORARIES

My life in politics has been worth it if only because I had the opportunity to meet the old man [Winston Churchill] in his various moods. And some of those moods were terrible.

September 2, 1967, *Star Weekly.*

I saw that house during the days of Churchill. I saw Churchill in that chamber in November, 1916, following Gallipoli, when he was in disgrace. When I first met him I said to him, "I saw you first when you were in disgrace." His answer was, "Which time was that?"

September 24, 1968, House of Commons.

Churchill's deputy prime minister of the war years, Attlee, formed a government which Churchill wanted to discredit. He said, looking at the front benches of the government, "It is a lousy government." Before the speaker could call him to order he went on to say, "I want to say that I was not using that term in an opprobrious way. It was purely a factual statement."

September 24, 1968, House of Commons.

Sir Winston Churchill had one political opponent who in debate it was said he feared above all others, Aneuran Bevan, the incomparable, a man with not Scottish but Welsh incisive wit. He passed away rather suddenly. Sir Winston was approached by his chief secretary who proposed that Sir Winston should say what was in his heart of hearts concerning his political adversary. The relationship between Sir Winston and Nye Bevan had never been of the very best. The press wanted to know what Sir Winston really thought of Nye Bevan. When asked, he said, "Are you sure he is dead?"

April 22, 1971, House of Commons.

Aneuran Bevan followed upon Winston Churchill, as he then was, and said, "I wish, Mr. Speaker, immediately to puncture this bladder of falsehood by the poignard of truth." They are words almost Churchillian in their import and power. Immediately someone wanted to have Mr. Bevan called to order, but he said, "I was quoting." As Your Honour knows, if an hon. member makes a quotation and applies it to anyone, no withdrawal can be demanded. For the next week or so there was a great deal of discussion in the letter press of the United Kingdom as to who was the author of those powerful words. Some said it was Shakespeare; although they could not find the exact quotation they knew it was there. Others said it was Beaumont and Fletcher. Others claimed it was some other Elizabethan dramatist. Finally two weeks later, when no withdrawal could be asked on a question of privilege, when he was making a further speech Bevan was asked whom he was quoting and he replied, "I was quoting myself." That is the parliament of the United Kingdom.

October 9, 1964, House of Commons.

[Churchill] was always a House of Commons man. His sense of humour, his ability in the thrust and cut of debate, devastating at times, was never wounding. Many examples of his wit are known to members, but the one which particularly appeals to me was in response to an interrogation received from a member whose legs were very short and who from time to time interrupted him. Sir Winston was in the midst of a speech, and his response was "The hon. member should not be so ready to hop down off his perch."

July 30, 1964, House of Commons.

I think of an occasion that I have never forgotten. It was at a dinner at 10 Downing Street. A lady, Mrs. Chamberlain, was sitting beside me. My wife and I were the guests. My wife sat to the right of Prime Minister Macmillan and to her right sat Sir Winston Churchill. He was very happy that evening and I

finally forgot myself to say to Mrs. Chamberlain, "He is very
happy tonight. He does not usually come out any more." She
said, "I am so glad. If it had not been for him we would not be
here."

March 14, 1966, House of Commons.

The President [Kennedy] is most impressive—a truly tremendous personality.

February 20, 1961, House of Commons.

The President of the United States has the kind of personality
that leaves upon one the impression of a person dedicated to
peace, to the raising of economic standards not only in his own
country but in all countries, and to the achievement in his day
of disarmament among all the nations of the world.

February 20, 1961, House of Commons.

Once in Washington, President Kennedy told me he'd caught
a sailfish. I said, "That's pretty good *bait*," and told about my
marlin. Well, that stuck in his craw. So when he visited Canada
one of the first things he said to me was, "Where's your marlin?"
When he saw it he said, "That *is* big," and then he added something revealing: "You know, I spent $50,000 trying to catch a
fish like that."

September 2, 1967, *Star Weekly*.

Whatever history may record of President Kennedy, his stand
on behalf of the equality of all men without regard to colour
was to me an earnest endeavour to bring about the culmination
of the dreams, the idealism and the life work of Lincoln. . . .
Whatever the disagreements, to me he stood as the embodiment
of freedom not only in his own country but throughout the
world.

November 22, 1963, House of Commons.

President Kennedy spent one million dollars and 400 operators
to defeat me in 1963.
January, 1973, *Maclean's.*

Throughout the years in which I have been in public life, my
course has not been directed to personalities or to building up
animosities against those on the other side of the house.
October 16, 1957, House of Commons.

I remember the election of 1935 when the Right Hon. W.L.
Mackenzie King, the then member for Prince Albert, ran on a
platform of "King or chaos." We got both.
March 10, 1971, House of Commons.

[On Mackenzie King]
You could never catch him: of course he was the hon. member
for Prince Albert. If you quoted anything that he had said, he
would tell you, "Read on." Sooner or later you could be absol-
utely sure to find the very reverse of what he had said earlier.
June 1, 1966, House of Commons.

Under the influence of fatiguing, long hours all of us develop a
shortness of temper which becomes national news. But this has
always been so. I recall one day particularly, July 28, 1941,
I think it was, when Mr. King was angrier for a longer period
than any other prime minister I ever saw.
July 21, 1960, House of Commons.

I remember very well when Mr. King defeated me in Prince
Albert in the election of 1926. The major part of his policy
was that he was going to reform the Senate. In sepulchral tones
he spoke of that body. He said, "We are going to put an end to
it." He secured the consent of everyone he appointed to the
Senate that they would agree to their own dissolution. When

in 1940 we asked to see those consents, he said they were personal. The only change was that he substituted live Grits for dead Tories.

October 3, 1974, House of Commons.

[Of Ian Alistair Mackenzie, Minister of Veterans Affairs]

Mr. Diefenbaker: All his life as long as I have known him he has been honourable and never right.

Mr. Mackenzie: I am glad that my hon. friend did not say that I was right and never honourable.

Mr. Diefenbaker: This is something I would not say. But I did point out that he had never been right.

Mr. Mackenzie: He has never lost an election in 30 years, which is more than my hon. friend can say.

December 11, 1947, House of Commons.

Mr. St. Laurent was not a spendthrift.

March 7, 1974, House of Commons.

[On St. Laurent]

If there ever was a Prime Minister of our country with a knowledge of the law to equal his, I am not aware of the fact.

November 21, 1949, House of Commons.

The Prime Minister spoke of the dangers facing this country unless the government were returned. When the C.B.C. news report concluded from the juke box came these appropriate words: "Drop that gun Louie, you are only fooling."

April 28, 1949, House of Commons.

In all the years I have sat in this house I have never had cause at any time to find that my right hon. friend [Louis St. Laurent] in anything he said to me told me other than the facts; and that is the highest tribute that can be paid to a political opponent.

October 16, 1957, House of Commons.

[On M.J. Coldwell, Leader of the C.C.F.]
I saw him but once when he became greatly disturbed at what
he considered actions dangerous to parliament. It was during
the 1956 debate on the pipeline. There is nothing more sacred,
as you know, Mr. Speaker, than the mace. It remains inviolate.
Only once, as I recall my history, was it ever grabbed by any
member of parliament. So disturbed was Mr. Coldwell that he
rushed up and grabbed the mace—a dramatic event that had
only been equalled in 1641 or 1642 when Cromwell grabbed
the mace at Westminster.
September 30, 1974, House of Commons.

Now take C.D. Howe. His views of parliament and mine were
totally opposed. He regarded it as an impediment to getting
things done. But we respected each other. Once in the House I
referred to "the sewer of his mind." The Speaker asked me to
withdraw the remark. I wouldn't, though I did point out that,
as a professional engineer, the honourable member undoubtedly
built a *good* sewer. But C.D. didn't bear a grudge.
September 2, 1967, *Star Weekly.*

Mr. Howe: My hon. friend is taking that from the sewer of his
own mind.
Mr. Diefenbaker: Mr. Chairman, that is a typically polite remark on the part of the minister, and I ask for an immediate
withdrawal of that statement.
Mr. Howe: In the last 8 years I have had probably more opportunity than any other man in public life to favour my political
friends and punish my political enemies, but never on any
occasion have I had an insinuation that it is a thing that I am
likely to do; and I will not take it from my hon. friend or
anybody else.
Mr. Diefenbaker: I am accepting the minister as being the
custodian of all perfection: Nevertheless, I want that statement withdrawn.
Mr. Howe: I will not withdraw it. . . .
[He finally does withdraw it]

Mr. Howe: I bow to your ruling, Mr. Chairman.

Mr. Diefenbaker: I appreciate that.

Mr. Howe: Just address yourself to the Chair, not to me; I am tired of it.

Mr. Diefenbaker: I am not talking to you.

February 16, 1948, House of Commons.

Day after day that is his [Howe's] one criticism, if we do not meet him with a spontaneity of praise that has all the appearance of a directed calisthenic drill.

June 22, 1943, House of Commons.

Mr. Diefenbaker: Now we hear the voice of the greatest parliamentarian of these times. He regards parliament as just a necessary evil. He regards the debates in parliament as worthless. That is his attitude.

Mr. Howe: It depends on who is debating.

April 20, 1950, House of Commons.

Do you not remember the pilgrimage made last year, when the Minister of Trade and Commerce [Howe] went down to South America? I sometimes wonder whether he was able to teach those dictators something.

February 15, 1954, House of Commons.

I have often thought of my hon. friend the Minister of Citizenship and Immigration [J.W. Pickersgill] as a "Gliberal." He would believe anything twice, as Mencken once said.

April 12, 1956, House of Commons.

It was an unusual speech. It brought the house once more back to the days when the ability to draw on classical allusions and quote from forgotten history was common. The house has lost that talent in recent years. The minister [Pickersgill] revealed

his erudition when he recalled the days of Boadicea. I could
not but conclude that his ideas of immigration were indeed
secured from those days when Boadicea lived in England and
did not wish immigrants from Europe to overrun that country.
February 17, 1955, House of Commons.

My hon. friend, the member for Bonavista-Twillingate [Pickers-
gill], would acquire an even greater reputation for wisdom if
he could for once maintain silence.
August 5, 1958, House of Commons.

This announcement by the minister [Pickersgill] is one that I
find difficulty in understanding. I am not now speaking of the
fact that the minister spoke in French, but of the content of
his speech.
August 5, 1964, House of Commons.

We all know that when the Minister of Agriculture [James
Garfield Gardiner] allows any of his powers to be removed from
him, especially in a bill introduced by himself, there is an
Ethiopian somewhere in the deal.
Some Hon. Members: Oh, oh.
May 30, 1955, House of Commons.

Kennedy has McNamara, and I've got McCutcheon.
1962. James Johnston, *The Party's Over.*

If I were a Roman Catholic, the first thing I would do every
morning would be to get down on my knees and ask my God
for absolution for ever having appointed McCutcheon to the
Senate.
1962. James Johnston, *The Party's Over.*

[On Leon Balcer, Diefenbaker's Quebec lieutenant, with whom he was not speaking at the time]
A second Sir George Etienne Cartier.

1964. Peter Newman, *The Distemper of our Times.*

The Bank of Canada, during the period when I was in office, had difficulties when Mr. James Coyne was governor. He had the idea that whenever he felt like it he could go out and deliver speeches which had a provocative, if not political, object in mind. He seemed to regard his position as that of a ministering angel whose words were infallible, and whose views were unchallengeable.

June 13, 1966, House of Commons.

[During the 1965 election campaign, this was a line Diefenbaker was tempted to use, but never did—publicly]
The papers say Dalton Camp is revolting. I cannot disagree.

James Johnston, *The Party's Over.*

[On hearing of the defeat of Dalton Camp in the 1968 general election]
Those who live by the sword shall perish by the sword.

Thomas Van Dusen, *The Chief.*

On L.B. Pearson:

I have not yet had the opportunity to pay my tribute to Right Hon. L.B. Pearson. We are often pictured as two great opponents. One would almost think that we were covered with the lather of personal antagonism. As a matter of fact most people do not realize the close relationship that prevails.

September 24, 1968, House of Commons.

. . . that adjectival authority, pusillanimous and uncertain as he pictures the darkness spreading over Canada.

November 1960, House of Commons. *Time,* December 5, 1960.

The Leader of the Opposition today put both feet down with boldness and imagination on both sides of several questions.

January 22, 1962, House of Commons.

After the Liberal Council in Ottawa last week, Mr. Pearson said, in effect: We're not going to tell you what our policy is until after the election! What a bold and imaginative policy!

February 19, 1963, Toronto.

Mr. Lesage recently described Mr. Pearson as a great diplomat, and it's true that the Prime Minister has diplomatically capitulated every time one has asked him to do something. If this is diplomacy, then I would have to agree with Mr. Lesage's description of Mr. Pearson.

November 30, 1963, Winnipeg.

The prime minister was caught by one of those machines [a tape recorder]. Then when they asked him about it, he said, "I didn't say what I said when I said it. . . . What I meant to say when I didn't say it was that I wouldn't have said what I said when I did say it."

1965 election campaign. *Maclean's,* January 1, 1966.

I could quote to the Prime Minister some of his really choice statements but I will reserve them until after he speaks so that I may be able to answer and fill in those parts of his speech that require to be elucidated in a straightforward manner.

January 20, 1966, House of Commons.

Leadership of a political party doesn't mean that you speak in words understood only by the so-called intelligentsia.

May 1, 1958, *Reporter.*

I can just see them sitting down together and the Prime Minister of Canada saying to Premier Lesage, "Now, what do you really want," and Mr. Lesage replying, "You know, Prime Minister, I have got nearly everything."

January 20, 1966, House of Commons.

When the Prime Minister of Canada went to Washington he was treated with about the same consideration by the president as his two dogs were except that he was not lifted by his ears.

March 21, 1967, House of Commons.

I first met Mr. Pearson in 1945 at the United Nations meeting in San Francisco and I was impressed with his personality. I have a great deal of respect for him.

September 18, 1964, Ottawa.

He contributes to the collapse of the whole moral fabric of the race he represents.

1965 election campaign, Hamilton. Peter Newman, *The Distemper of our Times.*

★   ★   ★

Every time I hear or see him [Paul Hellyer] in the house I am reminded of "The Deserted Village", the lines—
    And still they gaz'd, and still the wonder grew,
    That one small head could carry all he knew.
Every time the hon. gentleman speaks I think of Goldsmith.

June 6, 1963, House of Commons.

I love to make Paul [Martin] mad. You can do it by saying, innocently, that no other member has the ability to compress such small thoughts into so many words.

September 2, 1967, *Star Weekly.*

[Paul Martin] has an amplitude and felicity of phrase that makes it difficult on occasion to follow his exact meaning.

November 28, 1963, House of Commons.

I am sure the house listened with great interest to the Secretary of State for External Affairs [Paul Martin] as he reviewed the situation connected with this [the Columbia River] treaty— how, at his very best, in mellifluous words, he paid tribute to the Conservative Party as the government of the day which brought this treaty about. Indeed, if I may say so, Orpheus, with all his legendary powers, with all his ability to charm the birds off the trees by the sweetness of his remarks, would surely have paid a tribute in that connection to the Secretary of State for External Affairs had he been able to look down from above.

March 9, 1964, House of Commons.

To conceal thought he [Paul Martin] uses words. Indeed, as I listened to him from time to time I am reminded of someone in the United States Senate who described the tongue of a certain senator as being like a race horse: the less load it carries the faster it goes.

November 20, 1964, House of Commons.

Someone said some of his [Walter Gordon's] policies were pre-Keynesian. Some of them are pre-Cambrian.

April 28, 1964, House of Commons.

I do not want to interrupt the hon. gentleman [Walter Gordon], but I should like to say I have read everything he has ever produced and I will be looking forward to his new book. I read both for profit and for amusement.

April 1, 1966, House of Commons.

[Walter Gordon] has such wide knowledge that he used to take bankrupt corporations and turn them into corporations that were more bankrupt than when he started.

March 21, 1967, House of Commons.

[Walter Gordon] has gone abroad to deal with international affairs, a subject he has shown no capacity to understand up to the present time.

June 12, 1967, House of Commons.

As the hon. lady [Judy LaMarsh] only started as a law student, I am speaking over her head.

March 3, 1965, House of Commons.

Oh, ladies and gentlemen, you don't understand what it's been like in these last 2 years, sitting across from them—sitting across from all those men . . . and that woman.

1965 election campaign. *Maclean's,* January 1, 1966.

[Mitchell Sharp's] favourite sport is pushing people around and breaking the law.

1962 election campaign. *Maclean's,* July 28, 1962.

[Mitchell Sharp] still has that senior civil service mentality that affects so many of the front benchers of the Liberal party.

September 9, 1966, House of Commons.

All over the world people are laughing at Canada chasing after Mao and saying: "Won't you allow us to recognize you?" I can just hear the Secretary of State for External Affairs [Mitchell Sharp] saying, "Here I am, Mao, take me."

November 4, 1969, House of Commons.

The hon. member for Halifax [Gerald Regan] does nothing but engage in occasional desk tapping. It shows his intelligence that he makes that his major contribution.

November 26, 1964, House of Commons.

Favreau says he doesn't like me and I can think of no greater compliment.

October 21, 1965, Brockville, Ont.

I should like to hear from the Minister of Manpower and Immigration [Jean Marchand]. Five minutes are available and I know that in five minutes he will be able to tell us everything he knows about the subject.

December 19, 1966, House of Commons.

[The remark that inspired Lucien Cardin to mention the name of Munsinger]
I know the Minister of Justice [Cardin] is not acquainted with these things. He is seldom before the courts at any time, according to what I am told.

March, 1966, House of Commons.

[The following pun refers to Peter C. Newman]
I wonder where the Bouncing Czech is. Or maybe he finds all this beneath him, working with the peasants.

At the 1967 PC leadership convention. James Johnston, *The Party's Over.*

Mr. Diefenbaker: Peter Newman has a national reputation—
Some Hon. Members: Oh, oh!
Mr. Diefenbaker: —a notorious one for being a writer of fiction.
Some Hon. Members: Hear, hear!

July 6, 1972, House of Commons.

If Otto Lang had to cross a field with four cowpies in it, he'd manage to step in all of them before he'd make it to the other side.

January, 1973, *Maclean's.*

On Pierre Trudeau:

Have you ever seen him kiss a farmer?
John Robert Colombo.

As far as I am concerned, that represents his attitude to Parliament. We are tied up. We are nobodies. We sit, we speak, we are unheard and referred to as nobodies.
November 4, 1969, House of Commons.

The Prime Minister once said that as a student the person he most regarded amongst the statesmen of the world was the Italian dictator of many years ago. I will deal with that on another occasion when the Prime Minister is here. Subtlety, destruction, undermining deviousness, were the characteristics of that person.
December 13, 1968, House of Commons.

I have a volume here which describes Machiavelli as having been a talented dissembler, a ready opportunist, a master in the field of human weakness, an accountant of forgotten sentences, a promoter of vanity, a skilful juggler, a lover of cunning and a worshipper of force.
July 15, 1969, House of Commons.

I have in my hand a volume called "Machiavelli The Prince". The Minister of Justice [John Turner] is looking at the picture on it and he will see that it bears a striking physical affinity to his leader's appearance. In fact, if it were not for the identification and the fact that this is a picture of a death mask, frequent mistakes would be made by those who look at it.
March 31, 1971, House of Commons.

I join with the Secretary of State for External Affairs in extending deep and warm congratulations and good wishes to the

Prime Minister and his bride. I was surprised, however, that he made an admission that the cabinet was not consulted. . . .

The bride is the daughter of one of the most distinguished members this House has seen in my time. He was elected for the first time in 1940 during his honeymoon. Some years thereafter I recall seeing the bride of yesterday in the gallery opposite you, Mr. Speaker. She was then about 4 or 5 years of age. It was one of those occasions when there was an interruption from the gallery, dissimilar however from that which took place yesterday. In a voice which could be heard all over the chamber she said, "There's my daddy."

March 5, 1971, House of Commons.

I heard the Prime Minister. It was a four-letter word. It ended in 'k' and it wasn't 'work'!

January 1973, *Maclean's.*

The Prime Minister has had more holidays than all Prime Ministers since 1867. However, none has in fact been like the holiday he had in Switzerland. I saw a picture of the Prime Minister. He was mounted on a bobsleigh built for one. It was the first time in a year and a half that he was by himself. He did not have to turn and say "David, which way do we go today?"

March 7, 1974, House of Commons.

Speaking seriously about the Prime Minister's speech—I wish he were here; I know how busy he always is when I speak.

October 3, 1974, House of Commons.

Whom the gods would destroy, they'd first make mad with power.

May 27, 1975, House of Commons.

★ ★ ★

The hon. member for York West [Philip Givens] referred to
members of the House of Commons in terms of bovine anatomy
by saying, we are just as useful as an udder on a bull. I must
say that never has this Parliament received a more cryptic and
correct description than the hon. member's words the other
day. I am not acquainted with bovine peculiarities but taken
at face value, what he said indicated that, even though he is a
citizen of the city of Toronto, he knows his bull.

February 17, 1970, House of Commons.

Flora MacDonald is the finest woman to have walked the streets
of Kingston since Confederation.

January, 1975, Larry Zolf.

[September, 1967, PC leadership convention]
Stanfield, eh? He'll never be Prime Minister.

James Johnston, *The Party's Over.*

I never make personal allusions to any hon. member.

July 17, 1947, House of Commons (and ever since).

9 "I am a free Canadian."
DIEFENBAKER AND HIS PRINCIPLES

As long as there is a drop of blood in my body they won't stop me from talking about freedom.

June 3, 1962, Sudbury, Ontario.

I am the first Prime Minister of this country of neither altogether English nor French origin. So I determined to bring about a Canadian citizenship that knew no hyphenated consideration.

March 29, 1958, *Maclean's.*

I liken Canada to a garden . . . a garden into which have been transplanted the hardiest and brightest flowers from many lands, each retaining in its new environment the best of the qualities for which it was loved and prized in its native land.

Michael H. Marunchak, *The Ukranians.*

[From Diefenbaker's maiden speech in the House of Commons] The manner in which the census in Canada is taken prevents the creation of an unhyphenated Canadian nation. There is no question of the loyalty of those of German stock who were United Empire Loyalists, of those who came over in the forties, fifties, sixties. There is no question as to the loyalty of others, except the few who are today disturbing our unity and whose activities must be curbed. Other than those, the people recorded in the census as German are loyal to this country and intend to contribute to it of their best. My criticism of the census is that, regardless of the number of generations that have elapsed or the admixtures of nationality that have taken place during forty, fifty, seventy-five or one hundred and twenty-five years, so long as persons must register under the nationality of their paternal ancestor, there will never be that Canadianism which we wish to establish.

June 13, 1940, House of Commons.

We must dedicate our determination to encourage and develop in this country mutual trust and mutual tolerance. Above all, we must restrain the undermining of our Canadian confederation through encouraging or developing a dislike of Canadians of other racial origins, for Canada's destiny and Canada's future can and will never be achieved on the basis of racial prejudice.
April 2, 1946, House of Commons.

We have carried this question of racial origin so far that, if the Duke of Windsor had been in Canada when the last census took place and had had domicile by reason of his ranch in Alberta, he would have been required to register as a German.
April 30, 1946, House of Commons.

Civil liberty is not only the right of those who agree with us. It must be assured to all within the law, even though they condemn and oppose what we believe to be right.
February 19, 1947, Montreal, *Toronto Telegram.*

I have an intensive hatred for discrimination based on colour.
March 29, 1958, *Maclean's.*

In December, 1945, some months after hostilities had ceased and without reference to parliament, three orders in council were passed and declared to be valid by the judicial committee of the privy council, which would have exiled to Japan some 7,000 people of Japanese origin, a large proportion of whom were Canadian citizens. The fact that the privy council said that this could be done, that it was lawful, indicates the need of some restraining influence and the declaration of some principle to assure that there shall not be repetition in the future.
September 5, 1958, House of Commons.

I am a Canadian, free to speak without fear, free to worship in my own way, free to stand for what I think right, free to oppose what I believe wrong, or free to choose those who shall govern my country. This heritage of freedom I pledge to uphold for myself and all mankind.

July 1, 1960. From the Canadian Bill of Rights.

All societies need rules and symbols to express their highest hopes and goals. I view this bill of rights as a statement of a Canadian sense of history and of the objectives and standards that we accept in the fashioning of the society in which we believe. I know it has been said before by the cynics, who believe themselves realists, that declarations mean nothing. I have said before and I repeat: cynics have said for a thousand years that idealistic charters of freedom are meaningless. My answer to those who hold that view is that the same arguments could have been used against the sermon on the mount and the other great declarations of scripture when compared with the actual practices of those of us who are Christians. On the other hand, to what depths mankind would have sunk were it not for those supreme declarations of spiritual values which, touching the heart, cause man to know that there are things greater than materialism.

July 7, 1960, House of Commons.

Freedom grows in the practice of good citizenship. It withers or decays in the apathy or neglect of the citizens of the country.

July 7, 1960, House of Commons.

The principles of freedom are never final. Freedom is not static. It cannot be fixed for all time. It either grows or it dies. It grows when the people of a country have it in their hearts and demand that it shall be preserved. I would be the last to contend that any document made by man, however impressive, can assure freedom; but I think that what we have done will provide an anchor for Canadian rights. The ultimate assurance of them must always be a vigilant people, vigilant to invasions of and intrusions on their freedom; for, sir, when the spirit of freedom dies in the hearts of men no statute can preserve it.

August 4, 1960, House of Commons.

I know there are some who feel a sense of embarrassment in expressing pride in their nation, perhaps because of the fear that they might be considered old-fashioned or parochial. I do not belong to that group. I realize that a warped and twisted nationalism is productive of tyranny. But a healthy loyalty and devotion to one's country constitutes a most fruitful inspiration in life.

July 1, 1961, House of Commons.

Freedom is the right to be wrong, not to do wrong.

A favourite expression.

Canadians must unite in a national and personal dedication to obliterate anything in the nature of racial or religious prejudice.

March 24, 1952, House of Commons.

Freedom includes the right to say what others may object to and resent. . . The essence of citizenship is to be tolerant of strong and provocative words.

April 9, 1970, House of Commons.

The only effective answer to the propagation of false doctrines is to assure to every citizen information on what are the abiding principles of freedom. They will recognize their superiority over those false doctrines, those godless doctrines, those doctrines that would destroy the relationship between a man and his God and the sacredness of his personality.

April 12, 1948, House of Commons.

If we fail in our trust as wardens of the freedom of the world, we will have lost the opportunity which comes about once in five centuries. We will have lost the opportunity of building a better world.

March 6, 1952, Toronto.

We in the free world should explain our purposes, our ideals, our aims, to the non-committed world to a degree that we have not done heretofore. I found in my trip to Asia some years ago that too often the interpretation of what we stand for has been left to the whims of the communists. . . . I feel that today the ideals of the free world should be restated in simple terms so that all mankind will know that we have joined in a declaration of principles, and that all will recognize in these principles the equality of races and will condemn discrimination in any form.

May 19, 1961, House of Commons.

If ever there was a time that the commonwealth, with five to one of those who are members of the commonwealth being of coloured races, should do everything possible to assure freedom from discrimination, it is in our generation when the hearts of men are being mobilized and when the war of ideas is being fought as between Christianity and everything it stands for on the one side and communism on the other.

March 24, 1952, House of Commons.

A Damoclean sword hangs over the world. The peace which we fought for in two wars is fitful and uncertain. If the women could determine the future of the world there would be peace.

April 16, 1947, Montreal; speech to the Imperial Order of the Daughters of the Empire.

Idealism has its place . . . and if the free world sacrifices its idealism to godless materialism there will be little to choose between communism and democracy.

September 11, 1961, House of Commons.

Communism does not understand any other principle than
power. Communism does not believe in an immortal being who
determines the course of mankind, even though sometimes taking generations to do so. We do, and if we do our part now
without permitting ourselves to be intimidated, I think there is
a possibility that we shall be laying the foundations for a new
relationship between the communist world and the world of
freedom, a relationship which cannot hope to be attained if we
capitulate to the degree Khruschev asks us to. If we give up
our principles, what have we to live for in the years ahead?
September 11, 1961, House of Commons.

My prayer is that we will be directed in this matter. Some may
ridicule that belief on my part. I believe that the Western world
has been directed by God in the last few years, or there would
have been no survival. I believe that will continue.
January 25, 1963, House of Commons.

I left Mr. Louw [of South Africa] in no doubt that in Canada
there is no sympathy for policies of racial discrimination on whatever grounds they may be explained, and that such policies are
basically incompatible with the multiracial nature of the commonwealth association. I made it clear to him that the policy of
South Africa was a denial of the principle that human dignity
and the worth of the individual, whatever his race and colour,
must be respected.
May 16, 1960, House of Commons.

In the midst of the argument the day before yesterday, Dr.
Verwoerd [Prime Minister of South Africa] handed me a
clipping regarding the denial of admission of two negroes to a
hotel in the city of Edmonton. I do not think I have to make
any further observation in that connection.
March 17, 1961, House of Commons.

There were many who said it couldn't be achieved, but now we
have equality in Canada without regard to race, creed, or any
other consideration.

March 21, 1958, Welland, Ontario.

I have one love—Canada; one purpose—Canada's greatness; one
aim—Canadian unity from the Atlantic to the Pacific.

From nomination speech at the 1956 PC leadership convention.

We have a choice—a road to greatness in faith and dedication—
or the road to non-fulfilment of Canada's destiny.

1957 election campaign. Peter Newman, *Renegade in Power*.

In so far as northern Canada is concerned, there can be no
question whatever that in the territories there has not been a
policy of vision in keeping with the tremendous potentialities
of that area. . . . I can see this northland of ours with develop-
ments envisaged by D'Arcy McGee in his magnificent speech
at the time of confederation as he saw that great Canada. I can
see cities in Northern Canada north of the arctic circle . . . if
only the government would catch the vision of the possibilities.

February 11, 1957, House of Commons.

This is the vision. Canadians, realize your opportunities! This
is the message I give my fellow Canadians. Not one of defeatism.
Jobs! Jobs for hundreds of thousands of Canadians. A new
vision! A new hope! A new soul for Canada.

February 12, 1958, Winnipeg.

Canada must populate or perish—that is the answer. With such
great resources as we possess, and such extensive territory, we
can't survive with a small population.

April 18, 1958, *U.S. News & World Report*.

I forsee a Canada with 40 million population within the for-
seeable future.

April 18, 1958, *U.S. News & World Report.*

As I go across the country, I meet older Canadians as well as
the youth of our nation. I have always been very proud of them
and I am more so with the passing of days. They want to do
something for Canada. There are about 4 per cent who want
to create trouble, but the rest are motivated by tremendous
dedication to the building of Canada.

February 29, 1972, House of Commons.

We live in an age in which there is an increase in mob conduct.
I believe in the right of individuals to agitate for change, but
there is as vast a difference between agitation for change and
contempt for the law as there is between liberty and licence.
Organized anarchy, which is not being punished within our
country and except on very odd occasions is not being punished
in the United States, is dangerous to freedom. The right to dis-
sent must be preserved but the right to civil disobedience must
be frowned on.

January 27, 1969, House of Commons.

We live in an age that is becoming more and more permissive.
Some say there is no God, that each man should be able to live
his own life as he wills as long as he does so in private. I do not
find any support for that philosophy in the scriptures. The
Judaeo-Christian concept in the Old Testament is the foundation
of our religion.

April 18, 1969, House of Commons.

There is a movement within our country, as in other western
nations, of an underground nature, the members of which
masquerade above ground as crusaders for permissiveness, participate in campaigns for peace, and against the war in Viet

Nam. Their leaders claim that what they are doing is an exercise
in freedom of speech, when in fact it is often criminal and contrary to several sections of the Criminal Code. Violence begets
violence, and unless measures are taken to punish this kind of
wrongdoing those who advocate, support and engage in violence
will destroy the basis of our democratic society and pave the
way for absolute tyranny.

Today we find the youth of our country criticized. I do not
join in that. There are 2 or 3 per cent that preach revolution,
while the rest want to bring about change by democratic means.
Those who pretend that they believe in passive resistance or
disobedience as practised by Gandhi, are actually practising
revolution and advocating changes in our country on the basis
of revolution.

May 1, 1972, House of Commons.

[To a group of school children]
I only wish that you could come back when you're my age to
see the kind of Canada that you'll see. So dream your dreams,
keep them and pursue them.

1965, Taber, Saskatchewan. Peter Newman, *Home Country*.

"I will compromise on anything, but . . . "
DIEFENBAKER ON TRADITION

I want to make Canada all Canadian and all British!

1926 federal election campaign. Peter Newman, *Renegade in Power.*

Canadian unity is dependent upon the continuance of Canada as part of the British commonwealth. One could not imagine the various races and creeds in this country, the existence of rights and of responsibilities as between those various peoples comprising Canada, in any other relationship than within the empire, bound together in the empire by a spirit of loyalty and affection to the crown.

July 9, 1943, House of Commons.

British methods have worked through the ages and British methods will work today.

March 21, 1946, House of Commons.

No Canadian can but be proud that through the warp and woof of our constitution are the golden threads of our British heritage.

October 20, 1949, House of Commons.

The office of kingship is no mere formality. It is a symbol which binds us together. But in addition under our constitutional development, the kingship denies the possibility of there ever being a dictatorship so long as that kingship exists.

May 29, 1951, House of Commons.

Now they decide to alter the name "Dominion day" to make it "Canada day". It is not a fearful thing but it is indicative.

March 24, 1955, House of Commons.

This government, I say, is acting of its own accord, without reference to parliament or the people, to scrap the armorial bearings of this nation and remove all reference to the monarch.

October 19, 1966, House of Commons.

I would ask the Prime Minister why it is that Her Majesty, in her visit to Expo, Montreal, is to be denied seeing her Canadian subjects. A check with the state visit section reveals that no one will be allowed in the areas in which the Queen is during her stay there. I think this is a serious reflection on her good citizens of the province of Quebec. The arrangements should be altered so that these people, too, will have the opportunity of seeing their Queen.

June 22, 1967, House of Commons.

The expression "Queen of Canada" was first used by Sir John Macdonald more than 85 years ago. Some argue in favour of ending the monarchy. Sir, our freedoms, the rights of Canadians and in particular those of our compatriots who are French Canadian, were achieved by and under the British crown.

June 28, 1967, House of Commons.

With her husband Prince Philip and her children she represents to all the beauty and fullness of a family in the highest degree.

June 28, 1967, House of Commons.

I was shocked by the cartoon in the [Ottawa] *Citizen* showing Her Majesty the Queen and her husband. This is inexcusable and goes beyond the realm of what is fair and responsible when dealing with the Sovereign.

July 6, 1967, House of Commons.

For the last several years Young Liberal Associations and university Liberal organizations have been bringing out resolutions

to abolish the monarchy, and there has never been one word
of condemnation or disagreement from the Prime Minister or
any of the ministers of the crown. This is the kind of thing they
devote themselves to despite the economic conditions that
challenge this country and everything about it.

February 27, 1968, House of Commons.

Had it not been for the monarchy Franch Canadians would
have no rights today and would long since have been absorbed
by the United States.

November 4, 1969, House of Commons.

This government seems determined to abolish the monarchy.
Let no one deny that this is their purpose and objective.

November 4, 1969, House of Commons.

[Welcoming the Queen to Canada]
The Queen of Canada is a term which we like to use because it
utterly represents her role on this occasion.

October, 1957, Ottawa.

Every Father of Confederation including the French Canadian
representative, recommended or demanded the preservation of
the monarchy.

March 28, 1972, House of Commons.

On the pay cheques that are being issued now the Dominion
coat of arms has been removed. Is this another example of the
downgrading and chiselling away of our traditions?

May 3, 1972, House of Commons.

I will compromise on anything, but, speaking for myself, not
to the extent of the removal of the union jack from our national
flag.
November 13, 1945, House of Commons.

A flag that does not contain the greatness of your heritage is
no flag for a nation.
Gerald Clark, *Canada: The Uneasy Neighbor.*

One hundred and fifty years ago on my father's side my ancestors came to this country in order to seek freedom under the
union jack. My maternal ancestors came to the Red River as
Selkirk settlers. They came to this country which had as its
emblem the union jack.
November 13, 1945, House of Commons.

A flag design is not a trick by which one group imposes upon
others some evidence of a Canadianism that all will not accept.
June 15, 1964, House of Commons.

This question cannot have any other effect than to divide this
nation as it has not been divided.
June 15, 1964, House of Commons.

I ask you, how far are you going to be able to see that white
flag in winter?
June 15, 1964, House of Commons.

The flag has been made a party emblem, the Pearson pennant.
June 16, 1964, Winnipeg.

Does it move your heart to see this flag after it has flown for
a week or ten days? Does it touch you as freedom's banner stream-

ing o'er us? Does it consecrate in everyone looking at it the histor
the struggle, the strife that brought about our Canada? . . . . Sir,
a flag cannot be created by one man however powerful his
position. This is a time of instant creation but you cannot create
instant flags. Flags are born in the strife and turmoil of the clash
of history. They are not the result of an egocentric decision.
September 1, 1964, House of Commons.

God forbid that in this country we should apologize for stand-
ing for those things which made this nation great.
December 10, 1964, House of Commons.

I am never inclined to indulge in flattery, but Canada can never
repay the services rendered by the Royal Canadian Mounted
Police during the days of war, in preventing unrest in this
country.
June 27, 1947, House of Commons.

When I think of what the Mounted Police have done in Canada
I am reminded of the fact that we had no lawless west. When
the Fort Bentonese came over to Her Majesty's dominion to
whoop it up they came but once and then went back. I am reminded too of the Mounted Police corporal who met the Sioux
who had massacred Custer. There were two or three colonels
and a couple of hundred United States soldiers who had brought
the Sioux to the border where they were met by a Canadian
corporal. The colonel said to the corporal, "Where are your
men?" He said, "I am here—I will take them." Some of them
came to Prince Albert where they have lived ever since. There
was an authority, a greatness about that force.
June 26, 1967, House of Commons.

Today the Royal Canadian Mounted Police are losing some of
the greatness and grandeur of their past because to a growing
extent they are being used as traffic officers. I do not know

what it is but there is something that grates about seeing mounted policemen on duty as traffic officers.

June 26, 1967, House of Commons.

It has often been suggested that we should imitate the United
States system of government. I can never accept the concept
of the republicanism of the United States being made a principle or yardstick for a parliament in the British tradition. It cannot be done.

September 24, 1968, House of Commons.

Hon. members know what has happened recently in the United
States. Even making observations about it causes me very deep
pain. The President has been a friend of mine for years. I wonder how many people in Canada who were going to abolish the
monarchy are having second thoughts now about asking for a
president.

May 8, 1973, House of Commons.

11 "If there are statesmen here, they'd better resign."
DIEFENBAKER ON THE CONSERVATIVE PARTY

What I have tried to do over the years and since being chosen leader of the party is to bring together the people of all the races of men, to make it a people's party, a party for all Canadians.

Robert C. Coates, *The Night of the Knives.*

I am not a leftist but I believe that we should have a policy that is based, not on traditional, worn-out ideas, but on the needs of the nation today. We should see the youth of the country, and enlist them, before the party dies of hardening of the arteries. We should prepare to merit the support of those who return from overseas, for after all we got the majority of the soldier vote. We believe that we have a duty to uphold the morale of the people of this country.

May 30, 1941, Toronto, *Globe and Mail.*

The Church and the United Nations are fighting for freedom and security. Could we, as a party, find anything better to fight for?

June 6, 1942, Toronto, *Montreal Standard.*

The Conservative party will be the national party; it is the party which founded Confederation and the party that will save Confederation. . . . It is my intention to unite all Canadians from the Atlantic to the Pacific, under the banner of patriotism.

December 1956, PC leadership convention.

From now on, let us emphasize what this party stands for rather than what it is against. I want each of us to be dedicated to the welfare of all. It has been unjustly said that this party is the party of the big interests. The biggest interest of all is the welfare of the average Canadian and that is my main interest and the main interest of this party.

December 1956, PC leadership convention.

The poet Tennyson put it this way: "He is the true conservative who lops the mouldered branch away."
April 18, 1958, *U.S. News & World Report.*

The Conservative does not discard the experience of the past for the experiment of the present.
April 18, 1958, *U.S. News & World Report.*

From its beginning, our Party has steered a middle course between the extremes of unbridled individualism and state control. It has developed a philosophy of the responsibility of the Federal Government for the welfare of the nation as a whole and each individual citizen within the concept of the minimum of necessary government control or interference. The Progressive Conservative party believes in "change based on experience rather than on experiment."
May 26, 1962, *Saturday Night.*

How many of you realize this fact—that in 1965, out of the millions of votes that were cast, if, in twenty constituencies, we had secured 11,300 votes more, we would be the government of Canada today?
September, 1967, speech to PC leadership convention.

Some say, Let us go back to the good old days. I was there at that time. Not one Conservative from Quebec in 1921; in 1935, five; in 1940, none; in 1945, two; and in 1949, three. And then they say there's something wrong with Diefenbaker because he has more seats today than three leaders had in four elections.
September, 1967, speech to PC leadership convention.

[From Diefenbaker's speech accepting the leadership of the party]
I leave you with the message that raised the spirits of Canadians in the first great war. The officers were asked to do a formid-

able task and each one in turn, after having reviewed the actual situation, was fearful of the result and said it could not be done. Finally, the officer commanding said: "Now, gentlemen, you have given me every reason why it cannot be done. Now go and do it." My friends, let us unite and go and do it.

December, 1956, PC leadership convention.

The organized deluge of defamation and adjectival abuse that has been heaped upon the government of this country and myself as leader has never been equalled in the history of Canada.

October 2, 1962, House of Commons.

[To a Cabinet meeting]
If there are any statesmen here, they'd better resign. I want politicians!

Peter Newman, *Renegade in Power.*

To those of you who suggest I step down, I call to mind a statement once made by Winston Churchill—"I ain't going till the pub closes."

February, 1965, PC National Executive meeting. *Time,* February 19, 1965.

[After being booed at the 1966 annual PC meeting]
I read in the press that the old magic has waned. But I don't know how one could practise that with the trained seals that stood in front of me the other night and were placed there in advance.

November, 1966. Peter Newman, *The Distemper of Our Times.*

No leader can go forward when he has to turn around to see who is trying to trip him from behind.

November, 1966. Thomas Van Dusen, *The Chief.*

I underwent organized efforts to humiliate me at the annual

meeting of the Progressive Conservative party last November.
I have said nothing publicly about it but there comes a limit
to the continuance of the course of silence regarding that meeting that I have followed up to the present time.

June, 1967. James Johnston, *The Party's Over.*

As soon as I withdraw from the contest, I'm finished. I have
no further power in the Conservative Party. They can do what
they like then, and there is nobody to stop them.

September, 1967, PC leadership convention. James Johnston, *The Party's
Over.*

Always remember those who have on their shoulders the mantle
of leadership. They are subjected, and expect to be subjected,
to persistent attack. Don't, as the fires of controversy burn
round your leader, add gasoline to that fire.

September, 1967, speech to PC leadership convention.

You made that decision . . . of two nations. I hope you repu-
diate it before we leave here. I can't be interested, I can't be
interested in the question of leadership in this party under a
policy that is far-out Liberalism.

September, 1967.

I have always thought of an election as a great trial in which
the electorate listens to and weighs the evidence. I have found,
too, from my experience in previous elections that a reasonable
presentation of the facts and their significance must win the
verdict.

June 14, 1962, television broadcast.

12 "Throw the rascals in!"
DIEFENBAKER ON THE LIBERAL, NEW DEMO-CRATIC AND SOCIAL CREDIT PARTIES

You cannot beat the Grits by attacking them. I never use the word "Liberal" when I speak.

1957 election campaign. Dalton Camp, *Gentlemen, Players and Politicians.*

The [King] government has the billion dollar mentality.

House of Commons, July 10, 1946.

I do not see where the new provisions put many teeth in the law as it now stands. To me they look like false teeth.

July 2, 1946, House of Commons.

We should have an opportunity of having brought before parliament some of the invisible incognitoes who today dominate this government.

December 11, 1948, House of Commons.

No government in history—even the socialist government of Saskatchewan—has so far embarked on so many measures of a socialistic nature and a denial of free enterprise as has this government.

April 28, 1953, House of Commons.

There is no parliament today. With Howe advising the Prime Minister, we have the blind leading the blind.

April 29, 1957, Charlottetown.

Mr. Howe determines what is to be done. Mr. St. Laurent agrees. The rest of the cabinet says "me too" and the 187 other Liberals add "amen."

April 30, 1957, New Glasgow, N.B.

They [the St. Laurent government] were selling out Canada's birthright for depreciated United States dollars.

November 21, 1960, House of Commons.

The road of Liberal government leads to the extinction of parliamentary government in Canada.

1957 election campaign. *Time,* May 13, 1957.

[On Lester Pearson's debut as Liberal leader]
I listened to the Liberal convention. I heard Mr. Pearson's acceptance speech. I said to myself: "This is it. A want-of-confidence motion is coming." I waited that weekend. Then on Monday Mr. Pearson rose in the House. I said to myself, here it comes. But what did they say: "Give us back our jobs, but let's not have an election!"

May 1, 1958, *Reporter.*

There was a time when the Liberal government had great surpluses. How did they get them? By starving those in need, by starving the blind, and by starving those who were crippled.

February 8, 1962, House of Commons.

The Liberals are the flying saucers of politics. No one can make head nor tail of them and they never are seen twice in the same place.

May 5, 1962, London, Ontario.

They sabotaged your parliament with the deliberate intent of seeing that nothing was done. Anything that is good for Canada in their opinion is bad for the Liberal Party.

March 11, 1963, radio broadcast.

The Pearson policy is to make Canada a decoy for international missiles.

March 29, 1963, Kingston, Ontario.

You can be sure I will say the same thing everywhere in Canada.
I shall not employ the Liberal tactic of saying different things
in different places.
May 8, 1962, Rimouski, Quebec.

You will recall, Mr. Speaker, that the Prime Minister said the
other day that any time he wanted to call the President on the
phone he could do so. Any one of us could do that. The other
side of the question is that the President does not always answer.
October 21, 1963, House of Commons.

The heresy of yesterday is the Liberal orthodoxy of today.
A favourite saying.

[A suggested campaign slogan for the scandal-ridden Liberals]
Throw the rascals in.
1964 election campaign.

You cannot expect the Canadian people to be able to follow
the peregrinations of a government which started out with a
three maple leaf flag, said it was the only true Canadian design,
that it was based on history, heraldry, and structure, and then
changed its mind.
December 10, 1964, House of Commons.

I think it was the Minister of Justice [Guy Favreau] who said—
and I am sure he was not thinking of his own administration:
"The government of every people at certain times in their history is in the hands of near madmen."
March 3, 1965, House of Commons.

Socialism at its worst never equalled [Tom] Kent at his best.
No wonder they sometimes say that the Government is com-
posed of socialists in a hurry.
June 15, 1965, House of Commons.

They said pegging the dollar was an illegitimate offspring of mine, and now *they* claim its paternity.

October 22, 1965, Lindsay, Ontario.

A vote for this government is a vote for an open season for organized crime in Canada.

1965 election campaign, Prince George, B.C. Peter Newman, *The Distemper of our Times.*

[The Speech from the Throne] is a puerile, pusillanimous piece of repetitive propaganda.

January 20, 1966, House of Commons.

Never in Canadian history has there been a government so prone to be prone.

January 20, 1966, House of Commons.

The manner in which this thing has been presented has about it an odiferous aroma. . . . This thing is so smelly it requires no olfactory excellence in order to understand it.

February 10, 1966, House of Commons.

When I think of some of the statements made here I begin to think that we are living in a new age of palaeontology—political palaeontology—the invertebrate age, which is government without a backbone.

March 14, 1966, House of Commons.

If you ask this government what they are going to do, you get the stock answer that this matter is receiving the most careful and continuing consideration. One does not have to be bilingual to understand what that means.

May 26, 1966, House of Commons.

"Immediately"—a word which in the Liberal lexicon means "Whenever we think appropriate, however long the delay."
June 21, 1966, House of Commons.

Talk about a bigamous government—a government committing political bigamy. It is married to those who want an increase in interest rates and it is betrothed to those who oppose it.
July 5, 1966, House of Commons.

If only the government had 175 members they would be able to tell the opposition to take that course which my respect for parliamentary rules forbids me to mention.
September 8, 1966, House of Commons.

We have never before had a government which qualified to be called the "we-are-looking-into-it" government. Now we have.
May 10, 1967, House of Commons.

A few days ago, when dealing with pressing problems of unity, the economy, inflation, and other matters, the Prime Minister said: "I'm not disturbed." "Do not disturb" is all right as a slogan on a hotel room but it doesn't represent leadership for Canada. The other day he said, in a casual, off-hand way, "I'm not disturbed. Higher taxes are inevitable." And then he explained this away by saying it was anti-pollution measures that brought the situation about. The readiest and least expensive measure of that kind that I can think of would be to get rid of the present government at the earliest possible date.
September, 1967, speech to PC convention.

The just society: let us sum it up. It has given Canada the highest disregard for parliament in the lifetime of this nation. The just society has given Canada the highest spending, the highest taxes, the highest cost of living, the highest accumulation of unsold wheat, the highest neglect of the prairie provinces, the highest lack of consideration for veterans and their dependants and the aged. No one can deny that.

March 17, 1960, House of Commons.

There are so many of the intelligentsia, and I refer to them that way because that is what they call themselves—intellectuals— in the Prime Minister's office there is the suggestion that they are going to get a badge with "PET" on it so they will be able to identify one another.

March 17, 1970, House of Commons.

I have read that I don't like the views of intellectuals. That is one of several fictions that have been ascribed to me that are now almost legendary.

September 11, 1964, Fredericton, N.B.

The Liberal Party has become a hodgepodge of discordance, a cacophony of political nonsense.

June 4, 1962, Peterborough, Ontario.

Wherever one goes into the world today, people will ask you about the government of Canada. They ask: "Have you a hippie government there?" I have always defended it because I do not know the characteristics of hippies.

March 17, 1970, House of Commons.

The cabinet has been shuffled around. The Prime Minister took the deck and shuffled it. I have played cards from time to time but have never known anyone, however often he shuffled, who could turn four deuces into four aces.

February 29, 1972, House of Commons.

We have raised a standard of faith. The Liberals—if you can call it that—of fear.

February 24, 1958, Cornwall, Ontario.

I approach the altar of the Prime Minister's arrogance with great diffidence. The Prime Minister should treat the House with a little consideration and not try to be ingratiatingly contemptuous.

May 10, 1973, House of Commons.

The C.C.F. will not oppose these things; they accept these things, the setting up of boards, government by order in council, and the like, because in order to carry into effect the socialistic set-up which they believe necessary for the economic welfare of this country they would be bound to intensify far and beyond anything we have today the boards and controls already existing. That is the reason why they invariably support these things.

October 11, 1945, House of Commons.

I do not want to get into a controversy with my hon. friends of the C.C.F. in regard to matters of the imagination, because they are too highly qualified in that field, from their pictures of the new world that they envisage, for me to enter into any competition with them.

November 13, 1945, House of Commons.

The only thing in common between cooperation and socialism is the fact that a few years ago "cooperative" was made part of the name of the party to my immediate left. Cooperation is free enterprise.

July 10, 1946, House of Commons.

This morning the leader of the C.C.F. said that realism demands on occasion a change of viewpoint—and I thought, with what authority he spoke.

August 15, 1946, House of Commons.

The [C.C.F.] Government of Saskatchewan has not progressed beyond the four Bs—boots, buses, bread and one other commodity. Some people said there was a fifth B—Bunk.

January 30, 1947, Port Arthur, Ontario. *Globe and Mail.*

It has been very interesting to listen to my friends to your immediate left, Mr. Speaker, for they have endeavoured by constant repetition to delude the people of Canada into believing that they are in fact the true opposition because each and every one in that group speaks on each and every opportunity.

August 4, 1958, House of Commons.

As far as the New Democratic party are concerned the Liberals say "We are ready to merge with them, or at least to take them in." There is only one down there they do not want, according to the hon. member for Davenport [Walter Gordon], and that is the hon. member for York South [David Lewis]. He is a marxist, according to the hon. member for Davenport. The rest of them are all right.

February 5, 1963, House of Commons.

They say they believe in barking, but they must not bite.

January 20, 1966, House of Commons.

It used to be said that social security was a monopoly of the Socialist party: the two were regarded as being synonymous in the same way as in earlier days those who emigrated to Canada were told that here liberty and Liberalism were synonymous. They found that neither of these epitomies are well based in fact.

July 7, 1972, House of Commons.

In 1949, they elected 28 members. 37 years later they increased that by three. At that rate they should be able to elect a majority government by 2048. Even I don't expect to be around then.

January 10, 1973, House of Commons.

Do you have to be on the left to be moralistic?

October 4, 1974, House of Commons.

13

What could be more beautiful than the way the sky stretches
away to the horizon—gives a man room to breathe!

Thomas Van Dusen, *The Chief.*

It was so dry in Saskatchewan during the Depression that the
trees were chasing the dogs.

John Robert Colombo.

Those were the days when the only protection a Conservative
enjoyed in the province of Saskatchewan was under the provisions of the game laws.

April 29, 1966, House of Commons.

I ask the Minister of National Defence whether, in view of the
critical situation—I call it critical advisedly—arising from sub-
versive activities in Saskatchewan, he will consider the immediate recruitment to full strength of the Prince Albert infantry
and artillery units. Otherwise there will be no protection in
northern Saskatchewan against enemy activities.

May 27, 1940, House of Commons.

Until the farmer is assured of a fair return for his products,
the morale of western Canada will not be maintained.

November 19, 1940, House of Commons.

[James Ilsley] refers to the budget as a farmers' budget. No
doubt he has some reasons for making that statement. If I
understand it correctly it means this, that it is a farmers' budget
because of the fact that in the main it imposes increased income
taxes; and by reason of the operation of the policies of this
government and its failure to assure the farmer an income, there

being therefore no income, it is a farmers' budget for which the
government should be commended.

June 2, 1941, House of Commons.

To do something for Canada requires raising and continuing
to raise the standards of agriculture. Give the farmers the opportunity of obtaining the things they are entitled to.

September 26, 1945, House of Commons.

The solution for many of our problems would be for Canada
to have a population sufficiently large to consume at least sixty
per cent of our wheat crop.

August 15, 1946, House of Commons.

In this country, farmers were deluded over the years by the
plans of expert planners, but they are now beginning to realize
that the one party that truly placed before this country the
dangers inherent in a policy of control by experts was the Progressive Conservative party.

February 2, 1949, House of Commons.

It is true that there has been a fall in the cost of living. According to the department of statistics, the reason for that is that
the farmer is receiving lower prices.

March 10, 1952, House of Commons.

[On redistribution]
Let me now give you the picture as to how these modern Merca-
tors fixed the map. . . . There are not many Conservatives from
the West in the House of Commons. Apparently there are too
many in the opinion of those who drew the map.

July 1, 1952, House of Commons.

[The income tax inspectors] were so numerous in Saskatchewan just before the last provincial election that, rumour had
it, it became necessary for them to wear white badges in their
respective lapels so that one would not be chasing the other.

March 6, 1953, House of Commons.

The Canadian National Railways have found that without any
treatment the water of the North Saskatchewan river in its
present polluted condition is a very active agent for the removal
of scaling in locomotive boilers. That would seem to indicate
that it would not be too congenial to the health of human be-
ings.

February 19, 1954, House of Commons.

I must again urge the government to commence the construction of the South Saskatchewan dam and irrigation project.
We were promised it—I think the word was "immediately"—
in 1945. The definition of the word "immediately" in so far as
the Saskatchewan dam project is concerned closely resembles
our understanding of the meaning of eternity.

January 14, 1955, House of Commons.

I have heard it said that, so far as many of the high officials are
concerned, the Prairie Farm Rehabilitation Act could be defined
as patronage for retired, rejected, or resigned politicians.

May 30, 1955, House of Commons.

When there is no purchasing power among the farmers there
are no jobs in eastern Canada.

November 21, 1960, House of Commons.

I say to the Western farmer: "When did you ever have a government that was so concerned with your welfare?"

February 24, 1962, Edmonton, Alberta.

I saw the Leader of the Opposition [Pearson] on election night when he believed he was going to be occupying this seat. That is before the western farmer came in.

October 1, 1962, House of Commons.

When we came to office, as far as western Canada was concerned it was just another of those forgotten areas and the reason was simply this; that the Liberal party had reached the conclusion that the west would vote Liberal no matter how they were treated.

July 9, 1964, House of Commons.

We lost tremendously in population from the middle '40's until 1960, a period which happens to be coincidental with socialist government within that province.

April 29, 1966, House of Commons.

I remember the days when the Liberal party did not think that Saskatchewan was worth a dam.

June 7, 1967, House of Commons.

Why has there been such a reduction in the sum [of Federal tax money] given to Saskatchewan? What is the variety of abstruse mathematical calculation performed in the recesses of the Department of Finance? Why was this done? I would be the last to suggest that there were any political connotations or that the province is being penalized to any extent because of the last federal election.

June 12, 1967, House of Commons.

We are in a different position in the western provinces, apart from the great cities, from any other part of Canada. There are no criminal underground organizations in the smaller places in the country.

June 26, 1967, House of Commons.

I would ask the Acting Prime Minister [Paul Hellyer] to communicate with the C.B.C. with a view to securing an apology
from that organization for having described northern Saskatchewan as one of the most violent, hate filled areas of North
America. Would the minister have brought to the attention of
the C.B.C. that painting western Canada and its northern areas
as something straight out of the stone age, and without law and
order, is not in keeping with the Canadian tradition?
February 11, 1969, House of Commons.

We hear a good deal today about the Doukhobor problem. The
Doukhobors make good citizens; it is the Sons of Freedom who
have not made good citizens and who show no signs of doing
so. In the school where I taught there were 5 Doukhobor boys
who constituted the majority of pupils in that school. Three of
them became professional men. One became a leading artist and
the fifth became a missionary. That is indicative of what happens under our public school system. Those Doukhobors were
a good type and made good citizens.
May 22, 1950, House of Commons.

The law respecting Indians is a denial of the principles we accept
under the United Nations. As it is now drawn this bill places
these people in a position of wardship, making it impossible for
the individual Indian to preserve and protect his rights against
the tyranny of officials.
June 21, 1950, House of Commons.

I have known Indians over the years, since the earliest days in
the prairie provinces, going back to the days of Gabriel Dumont,
who returned to the area which is now Saskatchewan; I have
known of the Indians of the territorial days. They are a people
who are intensely loyal, and a people whose patriotic services
in two world wars have been beyond words of commendation.
May 6, 1955, House of Commons.

I think that is one of the major rights that the Indian tribes rely on, namely that in treaties that have been entered into as between their respective Britannic majesties and the ancestors of the present Indians, those rights are above parliament.

June 27, 1955, House of Commons.

This reminds me of one occasion when a certain politician in Saskatchewan was making a speech in a particular farm area. This was during the drought years when bullfrogs nine years old had never learned to swim. When his speech was completed he went outside to find out what the farmers thought about his farm program. In the darkness he heard one say to another, "Well, what did you think?" In reply he heard the other state, "He is a pretty good speaker, but an inch of rain would do a heck of a lot more good for us farmers."

June 23, 1966, House of Commons.

I might mention the historic nature of Prince Albert. I am not here for the purpose of advertising my constituency, but we are the only constituency in Canada that has ever been represented by three prime ministers.

April 29, 1966, House of Commons.

As Prince Albert goes, so goes the nation.

April 7, 1963, Prince Albert.

14 "Mes amis de langue français."
DIEFENBAKER ON QUEBEC AND MULTI-CULTURALISM

They said I was anti-Quebec, and I said to them, "Produce one line, one word that shows I was ever against Quebec." They couldn't do it.
February, 1964. *Maclean's*, March 7, 1964.

It is not being anti-Quebec to say that certain men have spoken in a way that cannot help but divide this country. Yet when one takes that stand it is argued that one is anti-Quebec. Not at all; I have never in my life uttered a word that could be so construed.
September 1, 1964, House of Commons.

I would like to make it perfectly clear that it is my conviction that it is essential for our party and government that the province of Quebec play a leading role in the Progressive Conservative party.
February 23, 1958, Trois Rivières.

We intend to unite this country. I went into the Province of Quebec and received a welcome the like of which I never received before.
November 5, 1965, television broadcast.

In 1922, when it was unpopular to take the stand I did, I took an appeal for French Canadian trustees against a conviction based on the teaching of French in the schools. It was an unpopular stand. It is the only reported case on this subject in the province of Saskatchewan. Of course it is one case to be remembered, because we who were counsel at the bar always remember the cases in which we were successful.
April 9, 1970, House of Commons.

Man for man and pound for pound our French-Canadian ministers are the equal of any that have ever occupied that position.
January, 1963, PC convention.

When I was Prime Minister I realized that French Canada was not receiving its fair share of appointments to the senior ranks in the civil service or in external affairs. One of the first directions given was that there should be a realization that those of French origin were not receiving their fair share of top level appointments, and action was taken accordingly. Furthermore, to make parliament bilingual, as it was under the BNA Act, we brought in the provision whereby simultaneous interpretation was adopted. These things had not taken place under Liberal administrations.
June 22, 1970, House of Commons.

It was upon my recommendation, and no one else's, that for the first time in history, the first time since Vaudreuil, one of French origin became the Governor General of Canada.
June 4, 1973, House of Commons.

They tell me I know nothing about the feeling of French Canada. That may be so, but at the worst of times, when I was leader we in this party elected more than three leaders had done in four successive election campaigns.
June 4, 1973, House of Commons.

I say to my friends in French Canada: the freedom you enjoy in our country came about because there was a British monarchial system.
September, 1967, P.C. leadership convention.

The leaders of the American revolution did not understand the French Canadian mind. They did not know that these people

were first and foremost Canadians. Whatever our differences
may be in this country, I belong to those who still contend that
that spirit is as staunchly held today as it was in 1776 and 1867.

November 19, 1963, House of Commons.

It was French courage and French valour that preserved this
part of North America for the British crown.

July 1, 1960, House of Commons.

[On the low enlistment rate in Quebec during World War II]
The people of Canada have a right to insist that there shall be
equality of service in all parts of this country.

February 24, 1943, House of Commons.

[From a pro-conscription speech]
I believe in the principle of Canadian unity, and I say that in
adopting a policy of this kind—one of not giving men in all
parts of Canada an equality of opportunity to serve—the Government is doing more to cause disunion and friction across Canada
than through any other act in the administration of the war
effort.

July 11, 1944, House of Commons.

[Prime Minister Lester Pearson] is having plenty of trouble with
his major supporter, the premier of the province of Quebec.
That premier [Jean Lesage] has decided what shall be done by
this government and this government has to be very careful that
it does not transgress in any way the ultimata that emerge from
the legislative buildings in Quebec.

June 11, 1963, House of Commons.

The suggestion has been made that I am anti-Quebec because I
dared to say that I disagreed with Premier Lesage. Is he anti-
Canadian because he disagrees with me? Was he anti-Quebec

when he disagreed with Premier Duplessis? Surely there must be better arguments advanced than that, that every time you disagree with the premier of one province in Canada you thereby become Anti-Quebec. I was never anti-Quebec at any time.

December 16, 1963, House of Commons.

I notice that the other day Mr. Levesque received the approval of one of the ministers of this government, who said he "stands for great things." Mr. Chairman, he stands for an associate state and a nation within a nation, something this confederation cannot accept and which would not permit the continuance in the next hundred years of this country in all its strength and its power.

November 27, 1964, House of Commons.

I cannot visualize Canada without French Canada. I cannot visualize French Canada without Canada. National unity based on equality must be the goal.

1965, Quebec. Thomas Van Dusen, *The Chief.*

I believe there must not be, as has been developing in this nation, first and second class citizens. That has been the trend as a result of all the discussion about associated states and a nation within a nation.

June 10, 1966, House of Commons.

I opposed the setting up of the commission on biculturalism. I said it would not work. To this day they have spent $7½ million and have divided this country as it never has been divided before.

May 10, 1967, House of Commons.

I stood against the Prime Minister when he announced the "two nations" idea. Laurier said it was wrong, Macdonald said it was wrong, Cartier said it was wrong, and every Prime Minister and leading French-speaking representative throughout the years has said it was wrong.

September, 1967, leadership convention.

The object of Confederation was not to produce Siamese twins in this nation.

September, 1967, PC leadership convention.

The adoption of the two-nations concept would segregate French Canada. I am not going to argue whether it's popular or not, to take this stand, to erect a Berlin Wall around the province of Quebec.

September, 1967, PC leadership convention.

To Quebec, they have promised everything under the sun. They have opted this out and opted that out. It's time that French Canada started opting in rather than opting out.

September, 1967, PC leadership convention.

We shall never build the nation which our potential resources make possible by dividing ourselves into Anglophones, Francophones, multiculturalphones, or whatever kind of phoneys you choose. I say: Canadians, first, last, and always!

June 4, 1973, House of Commons.

Bill 22, passed by the legislature of the province of Quebec, is now admitted across the country to be a knockout blow to national unity and to be unconstitutional.

October 1, 1974, House of Commons.

The bitter fruits of separatism come from the seeds that were sown in the twenty-two years of Liberal rule, when violence

was done to the Canadian Constitution and to the basic principles of Confederation, at a time when Canada's provinces
became the pawn of central government in Canada.

April,1963, *Saturday Night.*

We didn't have this division in the nation when we were in
office; we didn't have the country overrun with separatists.

1965 election campaign, Brockville, Ontario. *Maclean's,* January 1, 1966.

I have always taken the stand that separatism in Quebec was
not widespread, and the polls have shown it. To me one of the
most dangerous things today, and the most perilous to national
unity, is those people who, while condemning separatism, use
the fear of separatism as a smokescreen through which they
endeavour to advance their subtle demands for more and more
. . . . English Canada wants to bring about unity in Canada, but
to go on pushing through things regardless of the wishes of
English Canada and the multitudes of those of other racial
origins cannot but be serious to the future of Canada.

December 13, 1968, House of Commons.

[During the FLQ Crisis]
Would the minister consider mobilizing, with the assistance of
the Montreal police and also the Quebec provincial police, all
experienced members of the Royal Canadian Mounted Police
from across Canada so that there will be the fullest and immediate action taken? The Mounted Police always get their man.

October 5, 1970, House of Commons.

For over a year the government has known of these things. . . .
They could have been picked up a year ago on charges of sedition.

From the film *Action.*

The War Measures Act remains on the statute books of this
country. So long as it is on the statute books there is no reason
why governments, if they so choose, might not create emer-
gencies real or apprehended, thereby permitting them to com-
mit arbitrary acts under its powers.

May 7, 1946, House of Commons.

[Diefenbaker's first public French]
A mes amis de langue français, j'ai tenu à m'addresser à vous
dans votre belle langue maternelle, car il m'est difficile de
penser en français. Je vous remercie de votre indulgence, et je
vous dis merci . . .

1957 election campaign. Dalton Camp, *Gentlemen, Players and Politicians.*

[Speaking French] is a capacity envied by those of us who are
not possessed of it, and it is one that is of inestimable value in
understanding the aspirations not only of the race to which I
belong, but also of the French race whose contribution has
meant so much to the building of our country. I wish I could
express myself in French; although I understand the language,
I am afraid that if I tried to speak it the house would need a
translator to translate my translation.

March 9, 1950, House of Commons.

When I first came to parliament when anybody spoke French
everybody else left because they did not understand it. It was
slightly different when somebody spoke English but those who
were English speaking often left also.

May 10, 1967, House of Commons.

Apparently I just can't pronounce French well while talking.
An English-speaking friend joked to me, "I love to hear you
talk French on television. When you do, every English-speaking

person in the audience, who doesn't know a word of French, can understand every word you say."
April 1960, *Liberty*.

I understand what is said. When I try to reply, the quality of my French is such that nobody, from Vancouver Island to Newfoundland, who does not speak French understands. That is trilingualism, as practised in Prince Albert.
October 3, 1974, House of Commons.

[Diefenbaker's greeting to a boy who had been introduced by his father as "mon fils"]
Bonjour, mon-seer Monfils.
1965 election campaign, Quebec. Peter Newman, *The Distemper of our Times.*

I haven't practised my French. It's just that you are starting to understand it better.
August 23, 1965, St. Hyacinthe, Quebec.

You will admit that I am trying hard!
March 23, 1958, Sherbrooke, Quebec.

For the benefit of those who are not bilingual, I will now continue in English.
After a few words in French.

I recall the occasion of a state visit to Mexico when in the aircraft on the way down one of the officials asked me, "Have you got a speech ready?" I said, "No." So he got one ready for me. I studied it. I underlined it. I put marks here and there and other places. I delivered it with gusto. Afterwards on the way into the city of Mexico the chief protocol officer said, "That was a very good speech but we do not speak Portuguese

here." Then he added a tribute that I will always remember. He
said, "But you speak it with such a fine French Canadian accent."
March 26, 1973, House of Commons.

I am sorry I have never been able to learn the French language,
so as to make a speech in French. I do not have an ear for
sound. I am not like the Leader of the Opposition [Robert
Stanfield], who has a capacity of intonation which I lack. But
I would remind you, Mr. Speaker, that the Right Hon. W.L.
Mackenzie King, who was my member for years, only made
two speeches in French in his entire life. Once he said "Oui"
and the second time he said "Oui, oui."
June 4, 1973, House of Commons.

15 "Cooperation ever, subservience never."
DIEFENBAKER AND THE UNITED STATES

I am not anti-American. But I am strongly pro-Canadian.
July 13, 1958, *New York Times.*

We do not always agree with the United States, but our very
existence—with one-tenth of the population of the United
States, and possessing the resources that we do—is an effective
answer to the propaganda that the United States has aggressive
designs.
September 26, 1960, Speech to UN Assembly.

There is something about our relationship which might well be
a model for other nations in the world. . . . Where there is disagreement, we endeavour by mutual concession to arrive at a
basis of amicable settlement, thereby epitomizing something
which is so necessary in the world today.
February 20, 1961, House of Commons.

[Address to President Kennedy]
That you should have come to Canada on this your first journey
outside the United States since assuming the high office and
heavy burden of the Presidency, is further evidence of the en-
during friendship which prevails between the peoples of our
countries. . . . I assure you that nowhere will you receive a
warmer or more spontaneous welcome than here as neighbours,
champion of the rights of men, ally, and continental champion.
May 16, 1961, House of Commons.

We in Canada believe that good fences are necessary.
May 17, 1961, House of Commons.

tions. But it will not be pushed around or accept external domination or interference in the making of its decisions. Canada
is determined to remain a firm ally but that does not mean that
she should be a satellite.

February 1, 1963, House of Commons.

We do not need any assistance from the State Department, for
after all, I repeat, Canada is not in the new frontier of the U.S.

February 11, 1963, *Newsweek*.

Foreign investment should not enjoy a taxation advantage over
Canadians. If we allow an advantage to United States business
over Canadians, in this regard, we turn over to a foreign country
the control of our vast resources.

April 11, 1957, House of Commons.

We welcome any investment at all, from wherever it comes. We
just want Canadians to get the benefits of the riches of their
land.

July 8, 1957, *Time*.

If foreign investments are to remain predominant in resource
industries, Canada would tend to become a purely extractive
national economy.

August 5, 1957, *Time*.

There is an intangible sense of disquiet in Canada over the political implications of large-scale and continuing external owner-
ship and control of Canadian industries. The question is being
asked: "Can a country have a meaningful independent existence
in a situation where non-residents own an important part of
that country's basic resources and industry, and are therefore

in a position to make important decisions affecting the operation and development of the country's economy?

September 7, 1957, Dartmouth College, New Hampshire.

The degree to which U.S. industries have almost absolute power
and control over many enterprises in our country is not in keeping with Canada's destiny.

January 13, 1961, *Time*.

The United States is against the Canadians because they know
we are going to get into their markets now.

June 13, 1962, Brantford, Ontario.

Let it never be said that when a Prime Minister of Canada speaks
out for Canada he is against another nation.

April 5, 1963, Brantford, Ontario. John Robert Colombo.

The Prime Minister spoke in Halifax on October 22 and said,
"There is a continuing dialogue going on between the United
States and Canada." . . . Dialogue. When they went down there
a high official, speaking of the Canadian idea that was presented,
said, "Their ideas are screwy."

November 1, 1963, House of Commons.

Investment in Canada should be used by the corporations for
the benefit of Canada generally rather than be put at the direction of a country elsewhere, however friendly. That was our
view and our stand, and we maintained that United States investment in Canada should become Canadianized.

April 28, 1964, House of Commons.

We should not have police officers from a foreign country
wandering around in our country trying to find malefactors
[U.S. deserters] from their country.

November 23, 1966, House of Commons.

[On the takeover of the Mercantile Bank by the First National
City Bank of New York]
I can just imagine Rockefeller laughing to himself. "I came, I
saw and we conquered," that is the attitude of the Rockefellers
today.
March 21, 1967, House of Commons.

In the United States they got away from hyphenated consider-
ations. One never thinks of United States citizens according to
their racial origin. One never thought of Roosevelt as a Dutch-
American; one never thinks of Stassen as a Norwegian-German-
American; one never thinks of Eisenhower as a German-American.
While retaining their paternal love of their country of origin, a
common Americanism was achieved. That is what we are trying
to do in Canada.
April 21, 1950, House of Commons.

The recent gift of the United States of several hundred thousand tons of wheat has had a tremendous effect on the thinking
of the Indian people with regard to the United States, which is
sometimes described in Asia as being an imperialist country.
June 15, 1951, House of Commons.

We have to refrain from thoughtless criticism of the United
States, whose sacrifices and service in Korea for the preservation
of the principles for which the United Nations stand are im-
measurably greater than the combined activities of the other
members of the United Nations.
February 13, 1953, House of Commons.

I feel that in this country there is a campaign of anti-American
feeling, a dangerous luxury in the position in which Canadians
are.
March 24, 1955, House of Commons.

I sometimes think the major reason for the invidious attacks
that are made on the United States by certain people is that the
United States represents the greatest example of free enterprise
which exists anywhere in the world.

March 24, 1955, House of Commons.

One would almost think that the United States has become a
criminal in the dock. There are many things with which one
disagrees, but there is one thing that this House should not forget,
that is, that had it not been for the U.S. assuming the titanic
responsibilities that Britain had carried out for 200 or 300 years
without thanks, freedom today would not be in existence anywhere in the world.

May 1, 1970, House of Commons.

[On Vietnam]
Is it not possible, that if at this time the United States declared
an end to bombing for a period of two months as a beginning,
there would be laid a foundation from which the possibility of
peaceful negotiation might be the result?

November 24, 1966, House of Commons.

There are two battlefields today, one of war and one of ideology.
We do not convert people to think our way by pouring bombs
upon them, day after day and week after week.

November 24, 1966, House of Commons.

The United States should not have gone in there in the first
place, but they are in there and they cannot get out. To get
out would mean a loss of prestige and bring about the greatest
upheaval in Southeast Asia that has ever taken place.

November 4, 1969, House of Commons.

While there are people in Canada who advocate that the United
States should withdraw from Vietnam, to do so, in my opinion,

would be an act of retreat and surrender to the powers of communism and would mean the gallop of communism across Southeast Asia.

March 4, 1970, Purdue University, Indiana.

The Americans are in a desperate position in Southeast Asia. I do not think they should have gone in originally when President Kennedy, making one of his various monumental mistakes, moved in there with troops.

May 1, 1970, House of Commons.

[On Watergate]
The Americans, in attempting to get away from the British parliamentary system, made the president an all powerful king who might believe, as some of his predecessors did, that he is above the law.

October 3, 1974, House of Commons.

Nothing bordering remotely on what has been so far revealed in Watergate could happen under our system.

May 8, 1973, House of Commons.

Whoever has charge of commenting on the news controls the future thinking of the nation.
August 24, 1946, House of Commons.

How can we expect not to have anti-British feeling when we permit periodicals to enter Canada which attempt to destroy the morale of our people? Why should such anti-British publications as the *Saturday Evening Post* and the Chicago *Tribune* be allowed to enter the country? What is the use of having a department of information to furnish dependable information to the people if such information is neutralized, if not completely destroyed, by malicious articles appearing in these particular papers?
June 13, 1940, House of Commons.

It is through the instrumentality of the radio—and it is at least one of the main methods—that public opinion can be created today. The other method is through the press, and the government is trying to control the press.
March 25, 1942, House of Commons.

We in Canada are alongside the United States, and many programmes originating from stations in that country glorify crime and lawlessness. Our people are bound to be affected. . . . But we have a medium at hand [the CBC] to bring into the homes the necessity of obedience to the law, which if properly utilized would have the immediate and effective result of imbuing the people of our country with a greater appreciation for law and order.
August 24, 1946, House of Commons.

[On the CBC]
I believe there is being created in this country a monopoly which, unless it is restricted, will ultimately control the thought of this country.

August 24, 1946, House of Commons.

There can be no freedom of the press under autocracy, nor can there be autocracy so long as there is freedom of the press.

January 29, 1948, House of Commons.

Suggestions have been made that the C.B.C. news service is not always objective. I am not able to speak about the musical end or the drama end of the C.B.C., but as far as the news service is concerned I feel that year in and year out it is fair and reasonable in its objectivity.

March 31, 1950, House of Commons.

Why should seven foreign language newspapers in Canada, which go beyond the realm of freedom of speech, some of them advocating openly a change of government by force, be allowed to exist within this land with complete impunity so far as the government is concerned?

May 9, 1950, House of Commons.

We do not want to spoonfeed our people with the things that some board or group decides is good for the Canadian people. So long as it is not a matter of disloyalty, so long as it does not constitute sedition or is not contrary to good taste I can see no reason why various viewpoints should not be expressed.

June 28, 1951, House of Commons.

Reference to the Stars and Stripes and United States institutions on a programme going out over Canadian C.B.C. stations is something that I feel should not be permitted.

June 29, 1951, House of Commons.

The Toronto *Star* [is] a newspaper that seems to have an unusual capacity to think as the government is thinking.

March 24, 1955, House of Commons.

I can only say in so far as this [the Diefenbaker] government is concerned at no time has there ever been, directly or indirectly, any interference with the Canadian Broadcasting Corporation; and the nature of the observations made from time to time by commentators regarding this government and its undertakings since it came into power would be an effective answer to anyone who would suggest the contrary.

June 16, 1958, House of Commons.

The maintenance of the freedom of the press is never complete—it requires continuing and continuous vigilance.

September 22, 1959, Ottawa.

He [Tom Kent] is going to get all the papers in Canada under his control.

January 23, 1962, House of Commons.

Then we have *Maclean's* magazine. It is not regarded as one of our major friends, particularly since the editorial of June 27, 1957 which pointed out that the St. Laurent government had been returned.

October 2, 1962, House of Commons.

Satan saw my picture in *Newsweek,* and said he never knew he had such opposition in Canada.

March 22, 1963, Strathmore, Alberta. Peter Newman, *Renegade in Power.*

The *Newsweek* article was all part of a plan to destroy me. A man came from Washington and met with the Who's Who of the Liberal party. They planned that. They awaited that. It was conceived in Liberal headquarters in Ottawa.

March 14, 1963, Charlottetown.

The eastern magnates ran an editorial on the front page in
Toronto Saturday, saying they wouldn't support us. The only
reason they put it on the front page was because nobody
would read it on the editorial page.

March 26, 1963, Victoria. Peter Newman, *Renegade in Power.*

In this matter of defence it would have been so easy to have
done things that certain newspapers wanted us to do.

March 28, 1963, Toronto *Star.*

On the editorial page, they say don't vote for this government,
and on the financial page they say there is going to be the greatest boom in Canada's history.

April 4, 1963, Hamilton, Ontario.

The prophets are still at work, the polls are still being produced.
It is the best news I ever had. In two out of three elections
their predictions turned out to be wrong.

April 6, 1963, Goderich, Ontario.

More and more people are asking today, as they look at these
magazines [*Time* and *Reader's Digest*], why they should be
placed in an exempted position. I simply point out that nothing
has been done by this government which in any way indicates
that the great policy of Canadianization will go far enough to
ensure that Canadians will have the opportunity within their
own land to have their own magazines, unchallenged by unjust
competition from outside this country.

March 24, 1964, House of Commons.

The freedom of the press in a society of free men depends
upon commercial freedom of the press, freedom from direct
or indirect government subsidies or other forms of control.

June 15, 1965, House of Commons.

No Liberal newspaper dedicated to Liberalism could be so un-
objective as *Time* magazine has been.
June 25, 1965, House of Commons.

What about the C.B.C.? According to its programmes you
would think the United States was one of the greatest enemies
of mankind. It has even brought in Tim Buck and presented
him on television to tell Canadians what is wrong with the
United States.
January 20, 1966, House of Commons.

They [the Liberals] used the C.B.C. for political purposes during the last two or three days of the election campaign. They
spread propaganda across the country.
January 20, 1966, House of Commons.

Here is an article by Bruce Hutchison. No one can ever accuse
him of admiring anything more than he admires the present
government.
March 21, 1966, House of Commons.

I have nothing to say about the C.B.C. but this: I have found,
and this is regularly so, that whenever the government is in
difficulty there will always be available independent observers
of political thought who, free from any consideration except
the edification of the people and the purveying of truth, will
say, "After all, the government did what was appropriate."
June 21, 1966, House of Commons.

I now quote from a newspaper that worships at the altar of
Liberalism. I refer to the Winnipeg *Free Press*.
April 20, 1967, House of Commons.

Last night one of the reporters for the C.B.C. told about conditions in North Vietnam, confirming what Mr. Clark, the

assistant editor of the Montreal *Star,* had stated. No matter what is done the seeds have been sown by that broadcast and that article in the minds of the Canadian people to the effect that we in Canada are a variety of high class international double-crossers. We are accused of using our neutral position as a member of the international control commission to help the United States.

May 10, 1967, House of Commons.

The Toronto *Globe and Mail,* ever since the cancellation of the Avro Arrow and since they failed to secure a television licence in Toronto, has adopted an attitude of bitter criticism of the Conservative party. Yesterday, in an editorial vicious as it was vacuous, they denied the right of a member of parliament to advance in this chamber views that are not acceptable to that newspaper.

June 8, 1967, House of Commons.

To those that tell me that the Conservative party is in the doldrums—and some of them write this so often that they begin to believe it themselves—let me point out some facts. I do this, of course, knowing that you already have all this information but for some reason have forgotten it in some of the articles you write.

September 1, 1967, Ottawa.

You press people only know about ten per cent of the real John Diefenbaker.

September 2, 1967, *Star Weekly.*

Time magazine says: "Everything Liberal is fine." Oh yes, according to the Canadian issue of *Time,* not distributed in any other part of the world, everything is fine.

December 13, 1968, House of Commons.

It is as difficult to get information out of the C.B.C. in parliament as it is for a camel to go through the eye of a needle. They just simply do not give information. We pay and they advertise. Two or three people in the corporation believe they are above the law and they place before the people of Canada the kind of stuff that can only pollute the mind. If you destroy the physical being you are guilty of an offence. If you destroy the inner soul of the young men and women, boys and girls, of this country by this type of thing there is no offence under the present law as I see it.

January 27, 1969, House of Commons.

We pay for these revolutionaries to speak to Canadians.

March 25, 1969, House of Commons.

Many people are asking that the Don Messer show be continued, and they are not particularly pleased with the fact that Black Panthers and the like apparently have the inside track with the C.B.C.

April 30, 1969, House of Commons.

It has been interesting to read Mr. Weasel—Westell, I beg your pardon. That was a slip of the tongue.

July 15, 1969, House of Commons.

At any press conference, all the questions that anyone has in his mind or soul, I have always answered and I always will.

May 28, 1962, Prince George, B.C.

I have no statement to make at this time.

September 9, 1967, Toronto.

I like questions which are penetrating. They may hurt my political sensitivities at the moment, or those of the government.

But if you examine the questions asked on an average day, there is not one in a carload which would embarrass anybody.

December 7, 1962, *Time*.

[To reporters pressing him on his intention to run for the Conservative leadership]
Now there's a most interesting question; so novel, so unusual, it comes to me as a complete surprise . . .

1967. Thomas Van Dusen, *The Chief*.

[Typical evasion of reporters' questions]
For me to be able to instruct you in that would take a great deal of time.

Peter Newman, *Renegade in Power*.

17

"As Sir John A. Macdonald said . . ."
DIEFENBAKER ON SIR JOHN A.

Ah, but don't get me started on history, because then you shall know the meaning of eternity.

May 29, 1971, *Canadian*.

There can be no dedication to Canada's future without a knowledge of its past.

October 29, 1964, Toronto *Star*.

No one wants to go back to the days of 70 years ago when debate was unlimited. An example of that is to be found in *Hansard* in 1885 when the Saskatchewan Riel rebellion was being discussed. Speaking now from recollection, I think the first three speakers spoke from five to seven hours. One spoke for eight hours. Sir John A. Macdonald felt he could cover the situation and answer the arguments of the then opposition in a speech which he confined and repressed to five hours and 16 minutes. Those were the days when lengthy speeches were of the essence of debate.

July 12, 1955, House of Commons.

I've got a new Macdonald story. John A. was on a public platform with a Temperance person. And he said to the Temperance man, "Would you move away please, your breath smells terrible. . . . It smells of water."

September 2, 1967, *Star Weekly*.

Macdonald is as vital a personality today, as if he were alive.
He has been able to transmit his natural vision for this country
to all Canadian leaders who followed him, regardless of their
party.
July 4, 1959, *Maclean's.*

He was a wily fellow, Sir John was. Look at the pigeon-holes
in this desk! Guess that's where he used to hide the state's
secrets.
September 18, 1970, Toronto *Telegram.*

I look at this document I received from the office, and it is
similar to the kind of work one finds on John Macdonald's
copy of the original draft of the British North America Act.
That is one of the things that should be in the records of our
country. He did not write anything, but he did a lot of doodling.
He drew pictures of some of those who sat around the table.
He would have been a caricaturist or cartoonist if he lived today.
November 19, 1963, House of Commons.

We weren't always right. One time an Ontario leader came up
to Macdonald and he said, "You know, Sir John, I'm always
with you when you're right." Sir John told him where he might
go. "What I need is people who are with me when we're wrong."
September 7, 1967, PC leadership convention.

He knew what the public would follow.
January 12, 1969, Toronto *Star.*

This commonwealth means much to us because, after all, it was
a concept of Macdonald in 1864. He saw the picture of the development of the commonwealth.
October 2, 1962, House of Commons.

And, of course, there is Sir John A. Macdonald, the indispens-
able, without whom confederation never would have been
possible. No one denies him the title of the great architect of
Canadian confederation, except in some of the literature put
out by the Centennial Commission.

May 10, 1967, House of Commons.

Two weeks ago, I had a lake named after me. They never named
one after Sir John because he wasn't addicted that way.

John Robert Colombo.

He was never unduly elated by success and never too depressed
by setbacks. He was a pragmatist and dealt superbly in the art
of the possible.

January 11, 1967, Toronto *Star*.

I have never got around to handing out compliments when they
are not deserved. I think of Sir John when he was interrupted
once in the House: he had said something favourable about a
minister in the Mackenzie government, and the minister said,
"That is flattery." Sir John said, "No, it is a compliment." The
minister said, "What is the difference?" Sir John replied,
"Flattery is an agreeable untruth."

February 5, 1971, House of Commons.

This is an occasion when this nation calls for Canada first: one
Canada. That was Macdonald's objective. That has been mine
throughout the years.

September 1967, PC leadership convention.

Sir John A. Macdonald gave his life to this party. He opened
the West. He saw Canada from east to west. I see a new Canada—a Canada of the North!

February 12, 1958, Winnipeg.

Just as Sir John A. led in the securing of the west, so we must win the new northern frontier.

1958 election campaign.

When I decided to bring before the people of Canada a plan for the development of the north, it was ridiculed. Liberal members, including Mr. Pearson the then leader of that party, said we were going to build roads and railroads from igloo to igloo. Apparently he had been reading what was said in 1874 regarding Macdonald's plan to support the building of the CPR: the Minister of Finance of that day suggested that Macdonald was endeavouring to build railroads from wigwam to wigwam.

1972, House of Commons.

I say to my friends in French Canada, the freedom you enjoy in our country came because there was a British monarchial system. Our leaders believed it was the only way Canada could ensure its independence. They opposed republicanism, what they called "American domination." They decided to build a Canada here, Canada first, foremost, and always. So to each of you, I say I believe in a Canada—a Canada undivided. A Canadian I was born, a Canadian I will die. That paraphrases the attitude taken by Macdonald.

John Robert Colombo.

To say that a development such as the South Saskatchewan dam is not economically feasible is to forget the national policy of Sir John Macdonald which was followed throughout the years that he was in power. Alexander Mackenzie doubted that it was feasible to build the Canadian Pacific Railway. Sir John said it was feasible and indeed essential if we were to have the development that is ours today in the western provinces.

February 11, 1957, House of Commons.

Continentalism was preached in the days of Macdonald. He stood against it and assured us that Canada would be an independent nation.

October 28, 1966, House of Commons.

I cannot accept the fears of those who believe we must be subservient in order to be a good ally of any country in the world. Macdonald fought this battle. The great merchants in the city of Montreal in those days—not the French Canadians—had their views on this subject, that after all Canada would be that much stronger if it were joined with the United States. That was not Macdonald's view.

February 5, 1963, House of Commons.

I look at my hon. friends opposite, and they give the impression as they speak that only they have any affection for labour. . . . The very foundation of trade unionism was under Macdonald.

June 1, 1966, House of Commons.

I think of old Sir John A. Macdonald. His ministers left him. He fought on. My ministers left on principle. Today we are united.

November 5, 1965, Regina.

There were people of little faith in Macdonald's day, too.

March 31, 1958, *Time.*

I think cartoons serve a very useful purpose. I see all the cartoons. Macdonald used to say he had the ugliest face of anyone of his time, but if Macdonald could see the cartoons today, he would conclude that he's in second place. As for the critics, well, big-game hunters don't go after gophers!

September 2, 1967, *Star Weekly.*

Sir John won in 1887 at the age of 72. And then he won again at 76. I'm only 70.

September 18, 1965, Toronto *Telegram*.

I'm able to say on the basis of history that those who are the most maligned are the most remembered. It's like Sir John A. Macdonald said: "As a boy I used to look for apples in orchards. We always knew where to go . . . to the apple tree with the most sticks and stones under it. And there we would find the best apples." I know what he meant by that.

January 4, 1975, Toronto *Star*.

18 "Nothing I ever do is political."
DIEFENBAKER ON JUST ABOUT EVERYTHING ELSE

[A preface to uncounted numbers of speeches in the House]
I did not intend to join in this discussion, but . . .

[Standard reply to critical letters]
Dear Sir:
This is to inform you that some crackpot is using your name and has recently written to me over your signature, putting forth views so eccentric in nature and so much at variance with your usual logical style that the letter could not possibly be from you. I felt I owed it to you to bring this to your attention.
Thomas Van Dusen, *The Chief.*

I think of a Liberal leader in the United Kingdom. They called him the "chamber-maid." Every time he got up he emptied the chamber.
March 17, 1970, House of Commons.

I believe it was the Right Hon. Mackenzie King, in the election of 1935, who was visiting a certain province in which one of his grandfathers was buried. During the course of the day he said he would like very much to visit that cemetery. He said, "You know, he was a fine man but he was a Conservative; I never quite understood that. He voted Conservative consistently." The member, who afterwards occupied one of the highest positions on the treasury bench, stated, "Don't worry about that, Mr. King; he has been voting Liberal ever since he passed away."
December 16, 1963, House of Commons.

In so far as unemployment is concerned, the government has
been as idle as a painted ship upon a painted ocean. The Minister of Labour mentioned how good conditions were six
months ago. This reminded me of an old story on the prairies.
A man had died in a blizzard and sympathy was given to the
mourners by saying, "Just remember, six months ago yesterday was the hottest day of the year."
March 15, 1955, House of Commons.

I have never seen so many words chasing one idea in such a
way that nobody knows what the idea is. William Jennings
Bryan was one of those who used a multiplicity of words.
When somebody said he was going to be defeated in the election, instead of saying do not count your chickens before they
are hatched he said, "Do not compute the totality of your
poultry population until all of the manifestations of incuba-
tion have been entirely completed." That is an example of the
way this legislation is worded.
March 28, 1972, House of Commons.

It was in 1940, in a small town north of Regina. I was told
there was a lady in town, a very staunch Liberal, but she liked
me. So I went around to see her and then I said: "I see your
husband is on the voters' list too. Do you think he'll support
me?" "Why should he support you?" she replied. "He hasn't
supported me for five years."
April 2, 1975, Toronto *Star*.

[Concerning a bygone, hefty Conservative]
You could always tell how long he was going to speak. If he
folded his hands over his stomach, it would be brief. But if
he perched his stomach on top of the desk, we knew we were
in for a long one.
September 2, 1967, *Star Weekly*.

An under-endowed little college somewhere in the States had exhausted its list of wealthy alumni who might be tapped for a contribution in return for the bestowal of an honorary degree. So the Dean suggested: "I think we should honour that fine racehorse which has just won the Kentucky Derby; then we could ask its owner for the same large contribution which he made when we gave him an honorary degree." "Certainly not," replied the President. "A college cannot bestow an honorary degree upon a horse." "I don't see why not," replied the disappointed Dean. "We have often honoured a part of a horse."

Patrick Nicholson, *Vision and Indecision.*

There are only two species that actually go to war, men and ants. There is no possibility of any change in the ants.

March 13, 1964, House of Commons.

I do not know whether you have had anything to do with petitions, but I suggest you can get people to sign anything.

January 30, 1973, House of Commons.

If you say anything over and over again and it is false, sooner or later someone is going to believe it.

September 28, 1965, Brownsburg, Quebec.

You can't stand up for Canada with a banana for a backbone.

James Johnston, *The Party's Over.*

[A favourite quotation directed at the Opposition]
    A merciful providence fashioned us holler
     O' purpose that we might our principles swaller.

[Another favourite quote, usually directed at Liberal Members]
>   But man, proud man,
>   Drest in a little brief authority,
>   Most ignorant of what he's most assur'd.

[To a heckler in the House]
So far as the hon. gentleman is concerned may I say that I am reminded of the couplet:
>   As the cuckoo is in June
>   Heard but not regarded.

February 27, 1968, House of Commons.

As my hon. friend knows, the observations that one cannot hear can never be answered.

May 22, 1946, House of Commons.

Apparently what I am saying does not please the eggshell sensibilities of some of my hon. friends.

May 19, 1952, House of Commons.

When you throw a stone you always know which one it hits from where the howls come from.

July 11, 1963, House of Commons.

If intelligence were measured by noise, what brilliant people we have here.

March 29, 1963, Kingston, Ontario.

Interruptions of that kind result in no detour on my part.

July 7, 1967, House of Commons.

I do not understand this noise today. Apparently some of
these hon. members believe that if a gaggle of geese saved
Rome they are going to save the government by these un-
seemly interruptions!

February 6, 1975, House of Commons.

Had it not been for the trade winds between here and Newfoundland my great-great grandmother would have been born
in Halifax.

July 11, 1947, Halifax. *Maclean's,* March 23, 1963.

We have a national policy to develop the—what's the name of
your river here?—Oh yes, the Red Deer River.

October 14, 1965, Stettler, Alberta. Peter Newman, *The Distemper of
our Times.*

I am going to meet with the cabinet and I am going to watch
eventualities. . . . Eventualities are matters that arise and you
have to wait till they arise before you realize that they have.

April 10, 1963, Ottawa.

Criticism is sometimes necessary to create public opinion, but
use discretion.

June 9, 1942, Toronto *Star.*

I believe that what is being established is a new plateau from
which we will progress to greater heights of economic progress.

November 18, 1957, *Time.*

We know . . . that the way to prevent nuclear war is to prevent
it.

January 25, 1963, House of Commons.

Well, forecasts are always uncertain when it comes to popula-

tion. Increases depend upon a number of factors. Immigration is one, and another is the percentage of birth and death rates.
U.S. News & World Report.

Do not let us sound paeans of recession. Let us catch something of the greatness of this country. When we indulge ourselves and preach recession, it has this effect on the hearts of Canadians: it breeds depression. I am asking Canadians to come out of the valleys of doubt. I am asking this house to leave these valleys. Let us mount to the hilltops of determination and faith.
November 21, 1960, House of Commons.

My speech was very clear, very direct and very comprehensive. I do not think it requires any interpretation.
January 28, 1963, House of Commons.

I have no observations to make on that as far as press suggestions or ideas being expressed in that way are concerned. Further than that I don't intend to go.
December, 1958, Australia.

I endeavour at all times to refrain from statements containing implications.
April 18, 1958, *U.S. News & World Report.*

Nothing I ever do is political.
January 16, 1968, House of Commons.

I can talk to Him [God] in a familiar way and He hasn't objected so far.
January 10, 1973, House of Commons.

One of the things I very much treasure, is the Jewish people

of Vancouver giving me an award they call the "tree of life."
It's supposed to permit, or provide for, your living to be 120.
That ought to create some interest among some people.
February 10, 1968, *Star Weekly*.

I never evade a question.
April 2, 1952, House of Commons.

I have no competitor.
1963 election campaign. Pierre Sevigny, *This Game of Politics*.

My country has been good to me. I'm glad that I have lived in
this age.
September 23, 1967, Saskatoon.

Anybody can watch the parade. Those who make the contribution are those who get into the parade. The heavyweight
championship of the world can't be won by sitting in a ring-
side seat and handing out advice.
March 23, 1958, St. Hyacinthe, Quebec.

Some day I'd like to sit down for four or five days and tell the
stories I know. There are many things others have missed.
That's not egotism—that's fact. There are things no one else
can tell.
October 3, 1965, Toronto.

The last thing I want to do is to provoke controversy.
April 6, 1966, House of Commons.

I never think of memoirs. I'm still making history.
September, 1967, Peter Newman, *The Distemper of our Times*.

[On his proposed memoirs]
It will be a scorcher.

September 2, 1970, Toronto *Telegram.*

I never say anything provocative.

September 26, 1945, House of Commons.

A Note on the Sources

No other living Canadian has been more written about than John Diefenbaker, and the printed sources from which these quotations are drawn would fill several shelves. In gathering together the text of this book, however, I have tried to keep annotation to the bare bones, so as not to burden the reader. Still, I feel that I should explain my method and also acknowledge those books and authors I have found particularly useful.

In the text, my policy has been to include the date of utterance plus one source, though not necessarily the only source, in which the quotation was reported. For speeches made in parliament, I have used the text given in *Hansard* rather than in news reports, except when the latter sources proved pithier or more hyperbolic than the former one.

Among the books by or about Diefenbaker which have been useful are *Those Things We Treasure,* a selection of his speeches (Macmillan, 1972); *The Night of the Knives* by Robert C. Coates (Brunswick Press, 1969); *The Party's Over* by James Johnson (Longman, 1971); *Canada and Mr. Diefenbaker* by Burton Taylor Richardson (McClelland & Stewart, 1968); *The Chief* by Thomas Van Dusen (McGraw-Hill, 1968); *Gentlemen, Players and Politicians* by Dalton Camp (McClelland & Stewart, 1970); and the bibliot *Quotations From Chairman Diefenbaker* (Greywood, 1968).

Particularly helpful were two works by Peter C. Newman—*Renegade in Power* (1963) and *The Distemper of Our Times* (1968)—both published by McClelland & Stewart, as is Mr. Newman's 1973 work *Home Country,* which was also useful. Among other works consulted were *Vision and Indecision* by Patrick Nicholson (Longman, 1968); *This Game of Politics* by Pierre Sevigny (McClelland & Stewart, 1968); and *The Canadians* edited by J.M.S. Careless and R. Craig Brown (Macmillan, 1967).

Especial thanks are owed Doug Fetherling, who helped sort through enough material to make another book or two; and John Robert Colombo, who was unsparing of his support and his files and who demonstrated in his previous work the particular capacity of quotations both to enlighten and entertain.